MANAGING FOR
HIGH PERFORMANCE

MANAGING FOR HIGH PERFORMANCE

A Practical Guide

Roger Moores

The Industrial Society

First published in 1994 by
The Industrial Society
Robert Hyde House
48 Bryanston Square
London W1H 7LN
Telephone: 0870 400 1000

© *The Industrial Society 1994*

Reprinted October 1999

ISBN 1 85835 123 5

British Library Cataloguing-in-Publication Data.
A catalogue record for this book is available from the
British Library.

Typeset by: The Midlands Book Typesetting Company

Printed by: Optichrome Ltd

Cover Design: Pylon

Text illustrations: Sophie Grillet

The Industrial Society is a Registered Charity No. 290003

Ref: 991tw9.99

Contents

Preface

This book is for anybody who is accountable for the performance of other people besides themselves. It is intended to help leaders in organisations both large and small, in all organisations. It is not specifically addressed to any particular 'level' of management; high performing companies are not particularly interested in 'levels'.

Almost every book written about techniques such as total quality, continuous improvement and customer service strongly recommends that there should be 'commitment from the top'. This book is no exception, but there is a world of difference between 'commitment from' and 'reliance on'. Today's high performing companies are those in which people are set free to make improvements at all levels. It is in low performing companies that managers say things like, *'I can't communicate with my people until the leader has communicated with me,'* or even worse, *'I can't set targets until someone has set mine.'*

This book is intended to make managers at **all** levels think about performance management. If you are the sort of manager who needs to be spoon-fed with orders and instructions from on high, or needs a manual and a rule book to operate performance management, then this book is not for you; pass it on to your leader.

For decades the Industrial Society has taught the principles of effective leadership at work, and in this book the word 'leader' is intended to mean the person who is accountable for **your** performance or, if you like, the 'boss'. Everything in this book is entirely in accord with the precepts of action-centred leadership. The book should therefore be useful for any leader interested in improving his or her skills in:

- developing the mission statement;
- setting goals and targets;
- reviewing performance;
- one-to-one discussions;
- handling sub-standard performance;
- holding effective team briefings.

In addition some advice is given on supporting the goals of colleagues, coaching and training for performance management and some guidance on reward management.

We live in a competitive world undreamed of even ten years ago. This is the age of the high performing organisation, where the life of the low performing organisation is becoming ever more limited. So there is a chapter on the characteristics of the high performing organisation, which also discusses some of the competencies that need to be developed by the high performing manager.

If you are not, or not yet, the person at the top, you can still achieve considerable improvement in managing the performance of your own team or teams. Your success will benefit the rest of your organisation.

1

What is Performance Management?

There is nothing particularly new about performance management. It is simply a method of connecting your organisation's objectives to the people who are there to carry them out. It makes use of the procedures and communication drills you already have, takes into account your own culture, and establishes the key link between individual staff development and corporate goals.

It is a flexible concept, and organisations develop performance management programmes along different lines. However, most approaches tend to share the following elements:

■ A sense of purpose or mission which is understood by everybody in the organisation.

- Goals which are understandable and measurable.
- Developing targets which are within the control of the people they are set for.
- Regular one-to-one discussions with staff for reviewing performance, setting new targets, and staff development.
- Regular team performance reviews at which targets and goals are shared with all staff.
- Management and staff development based on the competencies needed to do present and likely future jobs.
- Based on the organisation's mission and future goals, developing a straightforward analysis of training and coaching needs for all staff.
- Rewarding people fairly for their achievements.

Summary

These are the main benefits an organisation could expect to derive from a programme of performance management:

- Keeping your goals and targets **relevant**.
- **Developing** all your employees towards achieving future business goals.
- Keeping your team briefings **relevant** and related to the goals.
- Providing **feedback** on progress towards achieving the goals.
- Helping to **analyse training needs** within the organisation.
- Keeping your **quality initiatives** (TQM, TQL, TCI, CIP etc) alive.
- Improving **appraisal** systems.

- Providing objective criteria for **rewarding achievement**.
- Making progress towards accreditation for externally measured **standards**, such as Investors In People and BSENISO9000 (previously BS 5750).
- Improving employee **communications**.

2

The Twelve Steps

If you are setting up performance management for the first time, or carrying out a review of your existing practices, you need to consider the following steps. They are set out in a logical order, but you don't necessarily have to wait for one to be completed before going on to the next.

Some of these steps may already have been taken, for example you may already have a mission statement (step 1) as a result of your total quality initiatives, and you may already have regular team briefings, the structure of which is the same as team performance reviews (step 6):

1. Develop the mission statement. But there is no need for everyone to sit back and wait for it. Nobody has ever suffered from incorrectly second guessing the Mission Statement!

2. Establish corporate objectives from the mission state-ment. At this stage think about the goals at lower

levels. Minimise bureaucracy. 'Continuous improvement' should be the keynote of the philosophy.

3. Formulate departmental goals in line with the mission statement and corporate objectives. Once again, nobody needs to wait for the message from on high, consult people and **involve** them in drawing up goals. Any subsequent adjustments to business goals will usually be minimal.

4. Establish key measures for the goals, and start setting individual targets.

5. Set up the practice of reviewing performance against the key measures. Establish the habit of regular (preferably quarterly) performance reviews, backed up by short but regular one-to-one meetings at all levels.

6. Set up team performance reviews in which managers share their goals and targets with their team members, which is what team briefing ought to be primarily about anyway, again at all levels.

7. At the same time draw up and develop the competencies (i.e. the behaviours or capabilities) required to achieve the goals of the organisation or the business unit. Use your organisation's own terminology. The job holders must be completely involved in this.

8. Cross-reference the competencies with the key measures that you formulated in step 4. This will help to review the key measures, improve the writing of job descriptions, and make sure that staff development is relevant to the needs of the business.

9. By now you will have a regular system of short performance management meetings in place (one-to-one and team), and can concentrate on the competencies and the actions needed to fulfil them.

10. Your management development programme can then

be drawn up, with full involvement of the managers concerned, based on the competencies identified as important for achieving the organisation's goals. Do not develop only managers; everyone can be developed.

11. A certain amount of training and coaching is needed. Some of this can be done by the organisation's own trainers and managers acting as coaches. People will need some coaching or training in:

- identifying measures, setting targets, individual personal development;
- how to run regular one-to-one performance reviews;
- how to run team performance reviews.

12. If it is your intention to link pay with performance, then you should by now be developing concrete data on which to design your reward scheme.

Important Considerations

Appraisal and performance-related pay

Everything we do should be related to our goals and objectives, and it makes sense to link the setting of targets and the development of managers to the overall aims of the organisation. Traditional appraisal systems, valuable though they may be, are not enough, and while we all know that incentives have their place, money alone never gets the very best out of people. If you have performance-related pay you need to make sure that it delivers something better than pay-related performance. I discuss managing reward in more detail in Chapter 13.

Leadership

Empowerment and facilitative leadership styles are the way ahead for all high performing companies, yet experience shows that there must be a set of simple drills through which leaders are recognised as accountable for the performance of their people, both as individuals and as team members. People must be set free and trusted, but at the same time you must manage the process, and not just by calling for the figures! Whatever the structure developed to meet the needs of the market – project teams, matrix structures, circle teams, etc, – there is always a basic need for accountability. Someone – the leader – has to set the task, monitor its progress and facilitate the development of individual employees. I discuss leadership and performance management in Chapter 12.

Job Descriptions

Clearly written job descriptions are obviously useful. Their value lies mainly in job evaluation, where they are used to help to establish equity between similar jobs for the purpose of validating basic pay or salary rates. They also help in recruitment and selection, staffing, organisational structure, training policy, appraisal and salary structure.

Job descriptions are undoubtedly valuable in managing performance, in particular the process of setting goals and targets. However, in a fast-changing organisation such as the typical high performing company, it is not easy to keep written job descriptions up to date. In a world where jobs change their nature and content so frequently, people do not see the need for constant redrafting. The written job description must not be allowed to dominate performance management. Keep them short and to the point, apply as little bureaucracy to the system as you possibly can, and review them about once every six months.

Total Quality

Too many of the otherwise admirable total quality programmes (which are usually accompanied by rather a lot of documentation) have actually taken 'ownership' away from the people whose job it is to do the work! This is not usually the fault of any particular scheme, but rather the organisation's perception of it. Companies have even set up Quality Departments, and appointed Quality Managers, when quality is obviously the concern of us all. Performance management will help bring quality to the level at which a continuous improvement can really take place.

While the corporate goals and plans constitute the 'output', the development of managers and staff acts as the 'input'. But you don't always know what you should put 'in' until you have at least a reasonable idea of what the output ought to be. So there is always a risk of setting the wrong goals and targets and establishing unnecessary training and development programmes, while neglecting the things you really do need! Performance management enables you to link your goals to your targets and to the development of your staff at all levels.

Consultation

Consult staff at all levels about performance management and how it is to work effectively. They know best about what is required: they know your customers and their needs, and have valuable knowledge about how their jobs should be done. Use your existing consultative machinery to develop ideas and suggestions for continuous improvement of the system.

This applies to all stages: consult on the mission statement, consult on your company goals (how many, how long, how worded?), consult on team goals, and make sure managers consult every individual on their targets whenever they are set or reviewed. If you intend to pay for performance, then consult all those affected on the scheme you propose, and listen to their ideas for implementation.

It may seem tempting to impose a scheme from 'off the shelf', perhaps something recommended by a management consultant. Consultants can be usefully employed, for their experience and their facilitative skills, but your performance management programme is yours; it belongs to you and your employees and to nobody else.

Summary

Twelve steps to performance management:
1. Develop the mission statement.
2. Establish corporate objectives.
3. Formulate strategies and lower level goals.
4. Establish key measures for the goals, and start setting individual targets.
5. Set up the practice of reviewing performance against the key measures.

6. Set up team performance reviews.
7. At the same time draw up and develop the competencies.
8. Cross reference the competencies with the key measures.
9. Check that regular one-to-one and team meetings are taking place.
10. Draw up management development programme.
11. Throughout the process carry out necessary training and coaching.
12. If appropriate design your reward scheme.

3

Mission and Vision

The Mission Statement

Many organisations have developed a statement of their mission in the past few years. Such a declaration is useful as a reminder to everyone what we are in business for. Because it acts as a reminder it is a good idea to write it down. The statement reflects the vision of the organisation and the fact that there is a sense of unity in striving to achieve the various goals and objectives.

A mission statement is more than a slogan; it needs to set out in very basic terms what the company is in business to do, and where it sees itself in the future. When you draw up your mission statement you must mean it otherwise it will be treated with cynicism by employees and customers alike.

The statement needs to emphasise the aim of providing service to the 'stakeholders' in the enterprise, which will certainly include the shareholders, customers and employees, and might usefully refer to suppliers, the environment, the community and the country. It should consist of between three and six short, clear sentences to which all employees can relate.

The mission can be a great motivator. But the statement is not! By itself – pinned up on notice boards with no other communication – it will probably meet a hostile response. But it is useful as a summary of the unified philosophy and culture of your whole organisation, especially if you are a conglomerate, involved in many different activities.

Many organisations sit down and review their mission statements every four or five years, to make sure that the words are still appropriate in a fast changing world.

The following example of a mission statement comes from managers and staff, The Performing Right Society. Note how it makes use of the organisation's initials to hammer home the message:

TO BE

Perceived as outstanding amongst international Music Rights organisations
Regarded by Members and Affiliated Organisations as an efficient and indispensable service
Seen in our dealings with music users as fair, prompt and accurate

---

Vision

The vision could be said to be the 'dream'; not a pipe dream, but a realistic long-term ambition. It may be argued that if everyone in your company has a clear sense of where it is going there's no need to write it down. But, particularly in large organisations, not everyone automatically shares the vision! So if there is a clear vision, something that can be said in one sentence, then commit it to writing, so that everyone remembers it, and newcomers are aware of it.

Summary

- Write the mission statement down – it is just a reminder of your mission and values.
- Make it clear and brief.
- If desired attach a statement of values and how they are to be applied.
- The statement looks ahead, not to the past.
- It must be truthful and credible.
- It's *your* mission statement and unique to your organisation.

4

Goals, Objectives, Targets

Terminology

'What's the difference between plans, aims, goals, objectives, targets etc?'

Every organisation has its doubters, and doubters usually thrive on confusion, so unless you make clear what the words mean you are likely to have to field questions like this when you begin developing your performance management programme.

However it is important that people understand the meaning of the various words used. The principle here is **use your own terminology**: there's no need to confuse people with new words unless they are absolutely necessary.

For example, in one engineering firm, the word 'goals' is not used. For the longer term aims, they use 'strategic objectives', and for shorter term aims they use 'departmental objectives'. It doesn't matter what words you use, so long as everyone knows what you mean!

There are no real differences between 'plans', 'goals', 'objectives' and 'targets' beyond those of scale. It may help to think of them as displayed like this:

From Goals to Targets			
'High' Level (Usually longer term)			'Low' Level (Usually shorter term)
Corporate objectives	Divisional Goals	Departmental Goals and Targets	Individual Targets

In this book we mainly refer to 'longer term' and 'higher level' aims as objectives or **goals** and 'shorter term' and 'lower level' aims as **targets**. If you are going to use new terms for the first time it is a good idea to produce a brief glossary like this one from a food manufacturer:

- VISION: Our ultimate aim.
- MISSION: The purpose for which we exist.
- VALUES: The beliefs we hold which guide our day-to-day actions and decisions.
- OBJECTIVES: The key overall objectives of the business – the object of our efforts which accomplish our mission and business plans.

cont.

- KEY RESULT AREAS: The means by which we determine our goals in terms of quality, output, costs, deadlines, people, customer satisfaction.
- TARGETS: The short-term actions which gauge our progress and when accumulated over time result in achievement of our goals.

So don't be sidetracked by arguments about words! Managing performance is all about breaking down your corporate goals, establishing key result areas at your own level, and setting targets which will enable each individual to play his or her full part.

Key Result Areas

We define our goals in terms of the key result areas. Some people call them *key headings, key measures* or *key values*. Once again, do not let problems of terminology get in the way, just make sure everyone knows what you mean.

The headings of your key result areas should reflect your mission and your business activities. They are a useful reminder when it comes to setting goals and targets at all levels. They also become your agenda headings for team briefings. Four to six should be enough. Here are some key result areas used by different companies:

- QUALITY, OUTPUT, COSTS, TIME, PEOPLE (STAFF), CUSTOMERS (food manufacturer)
- SHAREHOLDER VALUE, PRODUCT QUALITY, PEOPLE QUALITY, CUSTOMER SATISFACTION (motor vehicle manufacturer)

- QUALITY, COSTS, DEADLINES (TIMETABLES), CUSTOMER SERVICE, SAFETY (passenger transport)
- LEADERSHIP AND THE INDIVIDUAL, QUALITY CUSTOMER SERVICE, PARTNERSHIPS, TEAM WORKING (housing association)

Some of these words may have different meanings outside the particular organisation. What matters is that they are fully understood by everyone inside. If necessary define what you mean by them and put them in your glossary for everyone to see.

Rolling Down

As goals are 'rolled down' they are made more specific in different functional areas of the organisation. Goals set at the top give birth to targets for teams and individuals lower down.

Setting goals from top to bottom consists of these processes:

- Based on the company's mission and purpose, company goals with standards of measurement are developed. Up to twenty major company goals may be drawn up; more than this may be too many. Most organisations draw up goals on an annual basis, often as part of the general business plan. There is no reason why you cannot look further ahead, but the further ahead you go the more generalised the goals are likely to be.
- Each division or department develops its goals to meet those of the company. These are drawn up under the headings of the key result areas.
- Goals are set for each unit, branch or team in the

organisation, once again using the key result areas and setting out how the results are to be measured.

■ Goals (longer term) and targets (shorter term) are set for everyone, so that their personal objectives are designed to meet unit, departmental and company goals.

Underpinning all this is the process of continuous review of performance at all levels. The principle of rolling goals down into targets applies to all parts of the organisation, but obviously the number of steps in the process will depend on your size and the number of levels you have. However, even the largest organisation should not need more than five, perhaps six.

The achievement of the organisation's goals depends on a series of contributions made by each part of the business. It starts with the mission or purpose. But the goals provide much more than a general context for everyone's efforts. In performance management they drive everyone's key personal targets. This is done directly by a clear link between targets and business goals.

To facilitate the move from Stage 1 to Stage 4 we need a drill. This must be flexible enough to allow people to discuss and determine their own goals and targets at lower levels without necessarily having to wait for the final word from above. Then it needs to be flexible enough for people to make any adjustments later on if necessary. But it won't happen by itself everywhere!

The practice of rolling down goals into targets is hard work. It requires discussion, thought and flexibility of mind, and is best achieved by teamwork, with the relevant manager and his or her people working together. It can usefully form part of the process of installing performance management in a 'workshop' atmosphere in which managers together with their teams jointly thrash out their own goals and targets.

Summary

Here is a diagrammatic representation of how performance management functions from the top of an organisation to the lower levels:

PERFORMANCE MANAGEMENT FROM TOP TO BOTTOM

- MISSION AND PURPOSE
- THE COMPANY'S GOALS AND MEASURES
- DIVISIONAL OR DEPARTMENTAL GOALS
- THE KEY RESULT AREAS
- UNIT GOALS AND MEASURES
- YARDSTICKS OF MEASUREMENT
- INDIVIDUAL TARGETS
- PERSONAL OBJECTIVES
- REGULAR EVALUATION

5

Setting Goals and Targets for Individual Job Holders

Once divisional or departmental goals have been determined, the next step is to translate them into personal objectives for everyone. This process of target setting is the mechanism through which corporate goals are eventually achieved.

Breaking Down Goals

Goals Breakdown is the process of translating operational goals into personal targets at every level and for every person in the unit or department. The following example uses the theme of attendance rate to illustrate how this can be achieved.

Divisional Goal

■ Achieve attendance rate of 97% by 31 March this year.

Operational Level Goal

■ Propose action to reduce absence to the lowest level consistent with research into frequency, duration, date of absence with particular reference to the divisional target of 97% attendance.

■ Proposal by 15 December this year. Implement actions, when agreed, on 1 January next year.

First Line Manager Targets

■ Analyse absence by frequency, duration, date, by 15 November this year.

■ Review possible methods of reducing absence and calculate attendance rate with reference to the unit target of 97% by 30 November this year.

■ Carry out return to work interviews on the day of return from absence, from 1 January next year.

■ Establish sick reporting on the first morning of absence, from 1 January next year.

■ Communicate the emphasis on attendance to staff by 22 December this year.

Must people wait for goals and targets?

The process begins with the top management team and ends with those staff who have no supervisory responsi-

bility. But – and this may need emphasising – managers do **not** have to wait until their targets have been set before setting them for others lower down.   Listen, for example, to the view expressed by the Head of Supplies of Group Lotus:

> 'Maybe eventually we will receive the detailed goals from above, but meanwhile I set my own, and when they arrive from the top I bet they won't be too different from what I've set myself.'

Adjustments to targets can always be made once the pieces of the 'jigsaw' at the middle levels of the organisation have been put in.

Although commitment at the top is vital, do not fall into the trap of relying entirely on the 'top' to spoon feed communication down the line. Many attempts to improve efficiency fail because the organisation tries to 'cascade' goals down in such a way that at best people pay lip service to them and at worst fiddle the figures! In such a system people sit and wait first for the mission statement to be promulgated, then they wait for the corporate goals to be rolled down, and finally for their individual and team targets to be set, usually many months later.

Cascade can actually stifle the self generating initiatives characteristic of high performing companies. Little thought is given to making company goals relevant lower down, so people receive 'segments' or 'fragments' of the top goals, often expressed in statistical measures ('punctuality rates' and 'waiting times') that can have a wide range of meaning. No wonder they develop systems of 'managing by numbers'.

Neither should you allocate your company goals in equal proportion to all your departments, branches or business units. Developing goals lower down is like making a giant cake. You don't ask people to bring all the ingredients for a lot of small cakes; rather, depending on their resources (their specialities), they bring with them different ingredients to make up the full recipe.

The selection of personal objectives and targets should be relevant to individual jobs and not just a repeat of higher level goals, or an even smaller breakdown of them. In other words senior managers should not merely take their own targets and spread them around their staff.

Many business initiatives obviously require commitment at the top. But performance management requires more than this; middle managers are of vital importance. This is not to say that top managers have nothing to do, but by using the division or business unit as the 'pivot' of the system of performance management and management development works much more effectively.

Managers should look at their own priorities (targets) in terms of the key result areas (such as quality, output, costs, time, people, customer service), decide who is involved and how.

Always make sure your targets are in support of the corporate goals. Some targets may well support more than one.

Always discuss your targets and those of your team with your leader and colleagues, and of course always consult individual people before setting targets for them.

The Purpose of Targets

You may need to get managers to think about just what the overall purpose of targets is, and this is best done in your short workshops set up to introduce performance management (See Chapter 11). The obvious answer is 'to achieve the goals', but there are other reasons too. For example:

- To develop individuals, and progressively train them.
- To change priorities where circumstances dictate it without the need for 'panic' meetings.
- To encourage a continuous improvement of performance.
- To re-establish 'slipping' targets.
- To promote innovation.
- To broaden skills.
- To develop new areas of work.

- To achieve things that otherwise get neglected.
- To focus attention on priorities.
- To assist work planning.
- To improve job satisfaction.

Convincing the unbelievers

How do you get over the problem of those who argue that targets cannot be set for their jobs? There will always be some staff (and some managers) who say their jobs are entirely reactive; for example if they sit at a reception desk and greet customers; assemble components according to a pre-set programme; or sit by a telephone and wait for someone to ring.

It is vital that people – especially those at the 'bottom' in these routine jobs – know specifically what their contribution to the overall objectives should be, and setting goals and targets is the only way to achieve this. Thus management becomes 'pro-active', and over a period of time the successful achievement of individual targets leads to the realisation of company goals.

In the change from a reactive to a pro-active culture some staff will undoubtedly adopt a cynical approach to the idea of goals and targets. What are the objections people are likely to raise and how can we handle them?

Managers should be able to anticipate the following sorts of arguments:

- They are made to work harder for no extra money.
- They have had management responsibilities passed on to them including passing the blame on to them when it all goes wrong.

- Management has ridden roughshod over established agreements, custom and practice.
- Their time is wasted by requiring them to do irrelevant things.
- Management are always changing the goalposts!

Make it positive. A good method of opening the discussion when talking about targets for the first time with someone (and this applies at all levels) is to ask: *'What are the four or five points by which you would recognise whether you've had a GOOD fortnight/week or a BAD fortnight/week?'*

Typical replies might be:

- *'I didn't get any customer complaints.'*
- *'We had to change our programme half way through and lost production.'*
- *'The machine broke down and I lost bonus.'*
- *'We actually achieved a 100% customer satisfaction level for the first time this year.'*

People's experience of good or bad times at work nearly always relate to the goals of the company or business unit. Managers should be able to evaluate the response to the question in terms of the goals at business unit level, and in terms of things the employee can actually do something about.

Categorise the response in terms of the key result areas, and then move on to a discussion of targets in detail, reassuring staff, where necessary, that this is neither a mechanistic exercise nor is it designed to catch people out. If, for example, there is a company goal set in terms of the punctuality or attendance rates, it does not mean you will be fired for going sick!

Only the most cynical employees will say that it doesn't matter to them whether they've achieved anything or not in their work. Most people prefer to do a good job. Some may measure their success or failure in terms of personal rewards; don't put them down – we all work for money.

But high performing organisations are those that have a general idea of where they are going. Goals and targets are simply a way of setting sights on the future. In the real world we don't necessarily achieve some of them, while others are achieved a bit too easily. That is the reason for constant review and adjustment.

So if you are accused of 'always changing the goalposts' admit it frankly and hammer home the fact that we now live in a world of changing goalposts.

This pursuit of continuous improvement never stops. The perfect round of golf is eighteen. The fact that it is probably unachievable doesn't prevent people from constantly trying to improve their game. Much of the fun of golf – and other sports – lies in striving to achieve a better performance. The challenge for managers is to apply this sort of motivation to everyone at work.

Be firm if necessary. In the last resort people who remain unconvinced of the crucial importance of goals and targets may not have a future in a high performing organisation, and if, despite your best efforts, they remain genuine unbelievers you may have to develop fair and humane ways of parting company.

How to Set Targets

Remind people that in general goals are set at higher levels and are longer term objectives; targets, on the other hand, are short term, and once they have been achieved, other, new targets can be agreed and concentrated on.

Examine your own goals; ask yourself, 'What am I in business for?' Look at the key result areas of the work you and your team do in terms of **quality, output, costs, time, customers** (or whatever key result areas are appropriate for your organisation).

SMART targets

For many years the acronym SMART has been used to describe how goals and targets should be set. SMART means slightly different things to different people! Here we mean:

- Specific
- Measurable
- Achievable
- Realistic
- Time Related

When setting targets managers should bear the following in mind:

- What are the business priorities for the coming period?
- Who is involved? This has three elements:
    - things you must do yourself, personally;
    - things your team members must do;
    - things you must ask other people, e.g. suppliers, to do.

- What specifically has to be done to achieve your goals?
- By when?
- Which of the company goals do your targets support? (Remember that some of your targets may well support more than one company goal.)
- What 'customers' goals and targets must you support? (In other words what other departments need your support to achieve their goals?)
- What targets need you set to achieve your longer-term objectives?

Personal targets are most effective if
- they are quantified in terms of the key result areas;
- they are achievable, yet are set to **stretch** the job holder;
- they are set in areas within the **control** of the job holder and his/her team;
- they are consistent with the company goals and with the manager's targets;
- they are agreed with the job holder;
- there is a realistic timescale for completion;
- they concentrate on **things that must be done to improve performance** and are not just a list of routine or ongoing events;
- once they are achieved, new targets are set in other areas.

Yardsticks of Measurement

Every goal must be measurable. These measures can then be translated into targets which will consist of a specific set of actions. When determining yardsticks of measurement remember that there are many ways of presenting statistics.

Goals may be usefully put in terms of statistical measures but targets are best set in terms of actions which need to be taken. Here are some examples of measurement:

- Percentages/Ratios

  e.g. *'Attendance rate to achieve 98.2%.'*

- Frequency of Occurrence

  e.g. *'Hold a minimum of 10 meetings a year with your staff to review unit targets.'*

- Averages

  e.g. *'Achieve an average of 70% productivity by . . .'*

- Time

  e.g. *'Respond to call-outs within 1 hour of the first call, and 3 hours for additional calls.'*

- Prohibition

  e.g. *'No service cancelled for material shortage on planned work.'*

- External Standards

  e.g. *'Achieve favourable report from the Health and Safety inspector on his/her next visit.'*

  Here are some examples of good and bad targets:

BAD: *'Improve Customer Satisfaction.'*

GOOD: *'Identify one area of the Section's work with which a major customer is dissatisfied by.............(date) and produce a plan for improvement.'*

BAD: *'Establish close liaison with xyz Department.'*

GOOD: *'Develop agreed customer/supplier contract with xyz Department by.............(date).'*

BAD: *'Improve staff communications.'*

GOOD: *'Hold monthly meetings of staff starting on............. (date).'*

Some Questions Answered

When it comes to setting the specific targets, here are some questions managers will probably ask:

'How many targets?'

It varies, but if you set more than about six, success in all of them is unlikely. The number you set will reflect the difficulty and time span, but it is not necessary to spread them clinically over each key measurement. Attack the areas where the need is greatest.

'How much detail?'

Make them precise enough to avoid subsequent arguments as to whether or not they have been achieved! But you do not need to be so precise that they state the method as well as the goal. Allow scope for the job holder to exercise initiative.

'How long should each target last?'

There's no magic time limit, but always consider staggering the deadlines. Most of us only complete a target close to deadline and if all the deadlines fall at the same time, there may be not enough time for the job holder to concentrate on them all, and quality will suffer.

The time span could be anything from a day to a year (in which case you'd probably call it a goal or an objective rather than a target), but to maintain enthusiasm, shorter time limits are better. Lower down the organisation, the time limits will probably be between two weeks and two months.

'How difficult should targets be?'

Targets must stretch and challenge a person and give him or her a sense of achievement. But they must also be realistic. What may be an easy target for one person may be too difficult for another. If the staff member does not think a target is realistic, he or she is unlikely to tackle it with much commitment.

Remember that consultation prior to target setting is vital. You may need to tone down somebody's enthusiasm; some keen people are willing to set themselves targets that may turn out to be beyond them. It may then be up to you, therefore, to set an easier but more realistic target.

'What about changing them?'

Flexibility is important, but don't chop and change for no apparent reason. Managers are all too frequently accused of moving the goalposts. Do not drop targets in times of crisis; likewise never cancel your one-to-ones in times of panic. But when it is appropriate, be willing to admit that you may have got a particular target wrong, and then take the necessary action to put it right.

Of course other factors may change the priority of targets, making them irrelevant, too easy or too hard. Your job when faced with a problem is to identify what other actions need to be taken to overcome it, rather than undertaking a wholesale scrapping of targets.

Reviewing Progress

Individual measures and targets must be discussed regularly. So managers must set aside a specific occasion – at least each quarter – for reviewing the performance of each team member. Set targets at these meetings, but not necessarily all at once and review them at least monthly (many organisations specify a fortnightly review). Once a target is achieved another one can be set. So some targets can be short-term, others longer term. Reviewing performance against targets is discussed in Chapter 6.

The Paperwork

Keep the paperwork simple. The only documentation necessary should be one piece of paper on which goals and targets can be recorded, and which can be used for recording competencies and staff development. Keep two copies: one for the leader and one for the job holder. An example of a performance management form is at Appendix 5.

If you use a form, it is simply a tool to help managers and their staff record achievements and what has been discussed. Allow people to scribble all over it if they want to. It is their tool. They will probably need to start a new one at each regular review.

Consulting the Job Holder

Always consult the job holder. This should be a Golden Rule. You have little hope of achieving your goals without the cooperation of those who work for you. Managers still set the targets, but should always ask people what they think they can achieve. If you consult you will learn things:

■ The job holder actually knows more about the job than anybody else, and will frequently have ideas about targets.

■ You will get cooperation. Even if the job holder is reluctant about the target, the fact you consulted with him/her in a genuine way (always giving reasons for your decisions), will be likely to result in improved cooperation.

■ Consultation raises involvement. Provided the targets are realistic the job holder will have increased owner-ship of his or her work.

■ If you have any form of collective representation, whether it is union, non union or mixed, consultation with your consultative committee will supplement your discussions with individual staff members and is a valuable means of maintaining good employee relations.

Monitoring

When you have your one-to-one at which you set targets, tell the staff member how you are going to monitor him or her; in other words how you are going to review his or her performance. Job holders should not be taken by surprise, nor should they feel you are permanently spying on them! Establish a balance between setting them free and regular monitoring. Obviously you can leave some people for longer periods between monitoring than you can others. More challenging targets might need monitoring at more frequent intervals. Measurement is important, but there's more to monitoring than calling for the figures! This leads us into a discussion on how to review performance.

Summary

- SMART targets are:
  - Specific
  - Measurable
  - Achievable
  - Realistic
  - Time Related
- Examine your own goals; what are you in business for? Look at the company goals and your key result areas. What are the business priorities for the coming period?
- Who is involved?
  - You personally?
  - Your team?
  - Other people?
- How? What specifically has to be done to achieve your goals?
- By when?
- Which of the company goals do **your** targets support?
- What customers' (both internal and external) goals and targets must you support?
- What **targets** need you set to achieve your goals? Targets are set in areas of work which
  - relate to company goals,
  - are within the control of the person for whom they are set,
  - but are imposed only if necessary.
  - Remember you are seeking to focus on improvements, not just cover the job description.

If too many targets are set they are unlikely to be achieved, so set no more than six or seven at a time.

6
Reviewing Performance

Managers need reminding of the fact that we need to review our goals and targets regularly in order to be able to tell whether we are winning or losing and to assess the contribution people are making.

Performance review is about comparing individual achievement against the target. You need to check constantly on whether targets are being achieved and, indeed, whether you are setting the right ones. You can't do this simply by calling for bits of paper; you must have a structured discussion with every one of your 'direct reports'.

This should happen at all levels in the organisation, and take the form of one-to-ones to discuss performance, review targets, make adjustments where necessary, and review competencies (which we examine later in this chapter). Remember, if your staff don't achieve their targets, you probably won't achieve yours!

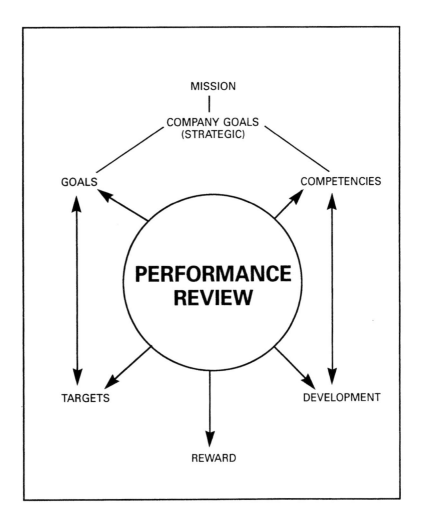

Fig. 1   Continuous Review of Performance is at the Hub of Performance Management.

The One-to-One

Throughout the year, hold regular one-to-one discussions with each team member to review targets and short term actions. These should be at least monthly, preferably fortnightly. This is perhaps where performance management is an improvement on some traditional appraisal schemes, which have degenerated into a somewhat bureaucratic annual ritual.

There is in fact a need for a more detailed review, an *appraisal* covering a longer period of time – past and future, at which the overall past performance of the employee is discussed together with action for further development. Appraisals are usually carried out annually, though six-monthly appraisals are not uncommon.

Monitoring and Review of Targets

Your review should take account of the following areas:

- Have the targets been met, and if so what can be learned from them?
- If any have not been achieved, why?
  - Failure on the job holder's part, e.g. leaving it too late?
  - Failure on your part, e.g. providing insufficient resources or not explaining the target clearly?
  - Circumstances beyond the job holder's control, e.g. sickness or extra work?
- If the target has not been met, should we extend the deadline or find alternative methods, or should we consider it irrelevant?

- How is the job holder doing in relation to the 'routine' parts of the job?
- Identify successes and failures, and set new targets as necessary. Be constructive at one-to-ones, and always put the emphasis on achievement rather than on abstract personal qualities.
- Good one-to-ones review performance and set sights on the future. Ideally they are short, agreed summaries of the working relationship between leader and job holder. There should be no surprises in a one-to-one.

Competencies

While goals and targets – the 'what to do' – constitute the outputs of a job, competencies are about job input – the behavioural 'how to do' skills. They are what people bring to a job, and are therefore important to the achievement of the organisation's goals.

Targets and competencies are closely linked. This is because progress against targets, whether satisfactory or not, is usually defined in terms of competency. For example, someone who keeps missing deadlines and losing documents, etc., may well have ineffective planning skills, a shortfall in competency which can possibly be rectified.

Assessing competency is about the improvement of individuals' and, therefore, business unit performance, and a valuable tool for individual development. Competencies need not be reviewed as regularly as goals and targets, except possibly by the training and development department. However, apart from the full scale appraisal (annual or twice-yearly, usually) these monthly reviews need only concentrate on those competencies which need to be improved.

Competencies are behavioural skills, which can be observed, evaluated and modified by development activities. They are not character or personality traits, and they do not measure 'attitudes'.

Competencies are useful in the operation of traditional appraisal schemes and analysis of training needs. Consulting as widely as possible, you must decide what competencies are required for each range of jobs, and you need also to be in agreement on the meaning of the words. Between ten and twenty competencies are about right.

Managerial competencies

Here is a list of possible managerial competencies, taken from the 'Personal Development' part of the performance management form used by a food manufacturer. In assessing the demonstration (or otherwise) of a competency you could use a rating scale (e.g. from 1 to 6). In this example, however, the manager (and job holder) are deliberately left with only three choices, to encourage a clear-cut assessment. This is not simply a 'ticks in boxes' exercise. It must be done with care, and any differences of opinion between leader and job holder about the display of competencies need to be discussed openly.

DISPLAYS COMPETENCE AT	ALWAYS	USUALLY	OCCASIONALLY
1. PLANNING			
2. SOLVING PROBLEMS			
3. BUDGETARY CONTROL			
4. SETTING OBJECTIVES			
5. FACE TO FACE COMMUNICATION			
6. WRITTEN COMMUNICATION			
7. DEVELOPING INDIVIDUALS			
8. TEAM BUILDING			
9. CUSTOMER RELATIONSHIPS			
10. SELF DEVELOPMENT			

There is not enough space in this book to describe the full meaning of all possible competencies, but here is an example of the definition of 'Planning and Forecasting' taken from a retail organisation, and drawn up as part of their programme of consultation with managers on the analysis of their training and development needs:

PLANNING AND FORECASTING

To be competent a manager must be able to:
- Handle and understand management data;
- Carry responsibility and accountability for all the assets under his or her control.

This will involve:
- Balancing the needs of the department with the overall needs of the company;
- Putting forward initiatives on the use of assets, property, plant, equipment, etc.;
- Chasing other departments who must provide input to obtain the required results.

Managers producing the best performance are those who:
- Identify the needs and resources that are required;
- Implement plans and control work;
- Take decisions on the deployment of staff;
- Minimise downtime, inconvenience to customers and loss of revenue;
- Plan and carry through medium and long term strategies to get results;
- Recognise the implications and knock-on effects of decisions;
- Turn overall objectives and standards into individual targets.

Non-managerial staff

Here is a list of possible competencies for non-managerial staff, taken from a firm in the engineering industry:
- knowledge of the job and understanding of what is required;
- quality of work;

- achievement against the targets set;
- relationships with colleagues;
- response to management/supervision;
- initiative and adaptability;
- motivation, drive and commitment;
- tidiness/housekeeping in personal and work terms;
- presentation in personal and work terms;
- punctuality and attendance;
- safety consciousness;
- customer relationships.

Summarising

Developing competency is not an attempt to produce a company 'clone'. It is not possible to standardise behaviour, and our ability to assess it will vary from one manager to another. Unlike some traditional appraisal systems this is not a score sheet!

If the primary purpose of this part of performance management is improvement (the process being designed to reflect the relationship between a manager and his/her staff) it doesn't matter if some managers mark 'high' and others mark 'low' because you are not comparing one individual with another.

On the other hand, if you are going to use the demonstration of competencies as part of your reward management system, then you must have agreement between managers on what the competencies mean, and on whether or not they have been demonstrated. Consistency is obviously required here, and this is where the 'leader's leader' comes into play as guide and coordinator.

It is not essential to cover every one of the competencies every time. Identify your priorities amongst them and identify the key half dozen or so. Any competency not important to the job can be omitted.

Clearly a potential problem occurs if the leader's assessment is considerably different from the job holder's. If this happens the manager should attempt to resolve differences of understanding with the job holder. But in the last resort, if agreement cannot be reached, then simply record that on this particular item there is a genuine disagreement.

Measuring and Developing Staff

Development of managers and staff is crucial to performance management because it is about continuous improvement. It is not just for the high flyers. Nobody is too old, too set in their ways, or too young for that matter, to be developed. Recognition of competencies possessed and those that need further attention helps people to achieve more against their targets and, in turn, helps you to identify people with the ability to do different, perhaps more responsible jobs.

Also by improving people's performance and competencies, development actions help individuals to realise more of their potential, which is both satisfying for the employees and beneficial to the performance of the whole organisation.

Self Assessment

First the job holder assesses him/herself on the competencies, concentrating on those that are relevant to the job. Then the leader goes through the same process, and the two of them have a chance to compare conclusions and plan the job holder's development in a rational way. (A good tip is to use different colours or symbols on the form used for assessment.)

The days of secretive appraisals are long gone, and a good thing too! The process of performance management depends on an honest self assessment by the job holder, not just of the achievement or otherwise of targets and goals, but also of the development of competencies, followed by a frank discussion with the leader.

Here is how job holders should assess themselves:

- Mark yourself honestly.
- Discuss it with your leader.
- Agree on it if possible.
- If it is not a problem do not waste time on it.
- If it is a problem decide together.

- If you are in difficulty, don't be afraid to seek specialist advice from the appropriate department (e.g. Personnel).

Self assessment against the competencies can be the 'fun' part of performance management. People should therefore not spend too much time on it!

Job holders should think of specific actions they have taken which demonstrate their use of the competencies. Only a few people 'over-assess' themselves; most of us have a relatively modest view of our performance. Indeed some employees are overly self critical at first, and these are perhaps the very people for whom performance management pays dividends.

Upward Assessment

How do you feel about your staff assessing **you**? In the drive for high levels of employee involvement, which goes hand in hand with the need for increased competitiveness, it is vitally important for managers to listen constructively to their staff. The use of consultative committees can be valuable in assessing employees' views of the performance of different departments (and by implication that of departmental managers), but what about inviting individual contributions from 'below' on how people evaluate the performance of their manager?

Judging managers on their 'style' may be an entertaining exercise for staff (though individuals are unlikely to be frank if their leader is an authoritarian), but experience indicates that management style is largely irrelevant. What really matters is whether managers achieve their goals and targets and the extent to which they use and develop their own competencies. It is here there may be scope for individual upward assessment as a means of improving the openness in communication between leader and job holder that is such an important characteristic of high performing organisations.

Currently there is an increasing interest in upward assessment, and some organisations have taken it so seriously that each subordinate is asked to complete an assessment of his or her leader. The results are collated by an independent person, e.g. a personnel or human resources manager, who chairs a special team meeting of the leader and those who assessed him or her.

It is probably best, at least in the early stages of a programme of upward assessment, to make it voluntary, treating it as just a form of personal communication between job holder and leader. Most advocates of upward assessment argue that it should be an anonymous exercise, at least initially, in order to elicit the comments of staff without fear of reprisals from their manager. Managers should then discuss the outcome of their upward assessment with the team. In this way, an atmosphere of honesty and trust can develop, and eventually lead to open upward assessment when staff can feel free to offer constructive criticism without fear of reprisal.

The Development Process

As we have seen performance management is really in two parts: the first part (goals and targets) is about the organisation, and can be regarded as the output; the second part (competencies and development) is about the job holder, and is the input.

The process is a balance between action needed to achieve the company's goals on the one hand, and develop job holders on the other. Obviously individual development must be relevant and related to the goals of the company.

The development of an individual is a continuous process, but there needs to be a formal appraisal, preferably twice a year but at least annually with the following basic points in mind:

- Identify needs and strengths (agree actions to develop needs and use strengths). Create situations and opportunities to practise competencies and continually coach, counsel and review targets. This will require that the manager work closely with the job holder.
- Not all development needs to be fulfilled by training courses. There are many development and learning activities which managers can arrange at less cost and more easily, quickly and effectively than training.
- It is more positive to talk about 'areas for development' than about 'weaknesses'.

To assess development needs it is useful to cross-reference the competencies required for the job (or a future job) against the key result areas of the organisation's goals. This chart is adapted from a consultative document produced by an organisation engaged in the process of analysing their training needs:

COMPETENCY	KEY RESULT AREA				
	Q U A L I T Y	O U T P U T	C O S T S	P E O P L E	C U S T O M E R S
1. PLANNING					
2. SOLVING PROBLEMS					
3. FORECASTING					
4. BUDGETARY CONTROL					
5. SETTING TARGETS					
6. FACE TO FACE COMMUNICATION					
7. WRITTEN COMMUNICATION					
8. DEVELOPING INDIVIDUALS					
9. TEAM BUILDING					
10. CUSTOMER RELATIONSHIPS					

This chart is simply intended as an aid to both managers and job holders in determining what are the important behavioural skills required to carry out the job. Where the competency in the row is important to the key result area in the column put a tick in the box. If you decide that the competency is fundamental to the job, then put two ticks in the box. Incidentally completion of a chart like this is a very useful part of training needs analysis for any job.

The development plan

Once development needs have been assessed, a development plan should be drawn up. This will comprise a set of actions designed to improve a competency which is weak or to consolidate one which is strong. It can also come directly out of failure to achieve targets. The plan should be made up of SMART development goals and targets: **what** will be done, by **whom** and **when**. Development objectives should be reviewed (not necessarily changed) at the same time as job targets – i.e. at least monthly.

If anybody should ask, 'Isn't this really the job of Personnel?' remind people that personnel and training departments are there to advise and help, but staff development is the responsibility of the staff member, assisted by his or her line manager.

ICL use a one page form specifying the job holder's development preferences and plans. Note that this form is owned by the job holder:

PERSONAL GROWTH PLAN			
CAREER DIRECTION (ASPIRED): FALLBACK DIRECTION: AIMING POINT:			
DEVELOPMENT NEEDS TO ACHIEVE AIMING POINT:			
RELEVANT EXPERIENCE FROM WHICH TO BUILD BRIDGES:			
EXPERIENCE PLAN			
Dates	Type of Role	Knowledge, skills, values gained	Experience gained
Owned by: Assisted by: (Manager)			

Fig. 2

ICL Personal Growth Plan

(From Performance Management – Managing Best Practice No 2 – The Industrial Society, June 1994)

Summary

The development process should involve the following steps:

- Identify development needs and strengths in relation to the competencies.
- Agree development actions for needs and strengths.
- Create situations and opportunities for practising competencies.
- Coach, counsel and continually review the development process.

Managing the One-to-One Meeting

The best one-to-ones are of course informal in style. But they are interviews, and require the appropriate skills. However since they are a regular and integral part of the way of life of the organisation it is suggested you refer to them as meetings or discussions.

A one-to-one has eight features:

1. A private, face to face discussion between job holder and the immediate leader.
2. The discussion reviews the whole of the job, not just a single aspect.
3. The meeting is structured, not just a casual chat.
4. The discussion includes past, present and future (up to three months in either direction).

5. The results of the meeting are briefly recorded in writing.
6. The discussion is two-way, that is, it's about the effectiveness of the job holder and manager as a partnership.
7. The discussion produces specific action points (e.g. revised or amended targets) with deadline dates. At the end of the discussion a date is agreed for the next one-to-one and this is entered in the notes.

The Format

The following points might help a manager planning a one-to-one, particularly if he or she is new to the procedure:

- This is not just a conversation but a meeting, with a specific aim. It therefore needs careful preparation and a structure. Work out in advance what you intend to say regarding all aspects of the review. But be prepared to modify your messages as a result of discussion and the input from the job holder. Ask in advance for a copy of the job holder's self assessment to guide you about his or her perceptions.
- Create the right atmosphere to relax the staff member. It should go without saying that the discussion be held in a quiet place, away from interruption.
- Both parties should take notes.
- REVIEW TARGETS: Discuss what has been done well, and what not quite so well and why.
- REVIEW COMPETENCIES: Link to achievement or not against targets and goals where appropriate.

- SEEK AGREEMENT: There has always been some debate on whether targets should be 'agreed' or not! Some experts say the 'A' in 'SMART' should stand for 'agreed', rather than 'achievable.' It is obviously best to seek agreement, because this ensures that the person will 'buy into' the target, and accept ownership of it. However, in the last resort you are the leader, and you have the duty to tell your staff member what you require.
- SUMMARISE at frequent intervals so you both know where you are in the discussion.
- SET NEXT PERIOD'S GOALS/TARGETS.
- Take a note of your discussion and let the job holder have a copy.

Some Interviewing Techniques

- In one-to-ones you should talk for approximately 20% of the time, and listen for the remaining 80%.
- Never criticise personality. For example, never say 'you are aggressive'. Quote examples instead: *'I am not saying you are aggressive, only that some of your behaviours mislead others into believing that you are – what can we do about it?'* Thus, always use behaviour as evidence of use or non-use of a competency.

When discussing development it is best to start with open questions, and invite the job holder's comments and feelings:

- How do you feel your job has been going since we last spoke?
- What do you feel you do best, and what do you feel you do worst?

- What are your strong points, and what areas of the job do you need development on? What particular problems have you come across? How do you think they could have been handled?
- What do you like best, and worst, about the job?
- In what ways could the job be improved? Have you any ideas? Is there any help you would like me to offer you? (In many cases you will not have to tell job holders about strong points and areas requiring improvement – they will tell you – and only as a last resort will you have to tell them.)

For more detailed information on how to conduct such interviews read the comprehensive guide, *Interview Skills*, or a shorter exposition of the key skills, *Interviewing*, both published by The Industrial Society.

Summary

A ten-point check-list on the basic skills of one-to-one meetings:
1. Even though you are planning a very short discussion preparation is vital.
2. Have you checked the records (if appropriate) of the employee you are interviewing?
3. Have you checked the facts of the employee's performance, such as goals and targets?
4. Have you worked out your main questions?
5. Are they mostly **open questions**, preferably beginning with WHAT, WHY, WHEN, HOW, WHERE, WHO?
6. Have you decided on your interview strategy, i.e. the order in which you will ask your questions?

7. Have you arranged the interview to allow enough time to cover everything you want to discuss?
8. Have you arranged the seating so that you and the interviewee are sitting in relaxed proximity to each other?
9. Have you got paper and pen conveniently placed to make brief notes without disturbing the interviewee?
10. Have you given instructions not to be disturbed?

8

Handling Poor Performance

What we perceive as poor performance by an individual employee is not necessarily the job holder's fault. In fact it is very unrewarding to think in terms of blame or fault in these situations, unless it really does turn out to be a case of misconduct.

It is all very well to review performance when all you have to do is compare what has happened with what you thought was going to happen! But the purpose of performance review is continuous improvement, so what happens if there is a shortfall? Or even worse, what do you do if the shortfall is consistent?

Most people say that poor performance happens either because the person can't do it (which makes it a training issue) or because they won't, in which case it becomes a 'rewards' issue. But there is a third possibility – you! A key part of performance review is your own performance; you are under scrutiny as well, not just when you've invited upward assessment on your own competencies, but also because of the way the jobs have been designed in your team.

Counselling

When poor performance occurs we need to adopt counselling techniques. This involves helping people to find out for themselves how to overcome work problems. Individuals are encouraged to think through their own solutions, including the changes they have to make to their behaviour. The manager's role as a counsellor is not to tell people what to do, nor even to provide gratuitous advice. Neither of these approaches will produce the lasting changes that result when people own a course of action which they have worked out themselves with the help of their manager.

If performance is apparently not up to the expected standard take the following steps:

1. What is the problem? Did we set the right targets in the first place?
2. Is the shortfall apparently caused by the person's behaviour – in other words s/he is not using the relevant competencies? Does it matter? If not, live with it, but the behaviour might make it difficult for the person to do a different job (perhaps at a higher level), making him or her potentially less flexible.
3. Hold your one-to-one discussion with the employee.

The right word in the right tone may be all that is needed, and will often be a more satisfactory method of dealing with poor performance than a formal disciplinary interview. The key skills of this kind of counselling interview are those of listening and questioning:

- Listen to any explanation, and observe carefully. Ask **open** questions to encourage the person to talk freely.
- Where an improvement is required make sure the staff member understands what needs to be done, and how his or her performance will be reviewed over the next two weeks.
- Arrange for a follow-up discussion to check developments.

4. Is it a lack of skill which seems to be causing the problem? If the person has done this job correctly in the past, consider whether refresher training is required. If the job is new to him or her, training or coaching is almost certainly required. It may be that the person is skilled enough in the work but does not get enough practice, in which case provide practice, and also monitor the person's progress.

5. Is the job right? The shortcoming in performance may be nothing to do with the employee: the job may have been badly designed, in which case you must redesign, and arrange for retraining if necessary.

6. If the person obviously has the skills to do the job but is not exercising them to your satisfaction it is probably a 'rewards' issue. We all get rewarded at work in one way or another, but sometimes the rewards are the opposite of what the organisation intends.

Example

Consider the case of two people and a leader. One of the two is very good and so the leader gives that person all the work, knowing that it will get done. Meanwhile the poor performer sits back and does nothing. The outcome is that good performance gets rewarded with more work and the bad performance gets rewarded with free time!

---

7. If the person feels penalised or handicapped for doing the right thing, you must act to remove these penalties. Likewise if the person is rewarded for doing the wrong thing – and this occasionally happens when people may produce good work but completely ignore their targets

- you must create positive outcomes for producing good performance.

8. Does the person feel that it doesn't matter? Have you hammered home the importance of goals and targets, or left them vague and somehow regarded them as a voluntary activity?

9. Check tactfully whether any obstacles have been placed in the way of a person's performance, perhaps by colleagues or by domestic and personal circumstances.

10. When you have investigated poor performance thoroughly and there is still no improvement, and there is no suitable alternative work available you may, of course, dismiss someone, but you must do this fairly and only after strict adherence to the organisation's disciplinary procedure. It is important to decide whether the poor performance is due to the person's incapability or to his or her misconduct, because the action you take in each case is different. Do not forget to follow the correct procedure, allowing the employee the right to be accompanied at each stage, and the right of appeal against the decision to dismiss. You may need to seek advice from your personnel or human resources specialists when taking this course.

Finally while it is important to keep a note of all your one-to-one discussions, it is even more so when it is a counselling interview of this nature, because your notes could be used as evidence if the matter is taken out of your hands.

Handling Failure

When goals and targets are not met, all your leadership skills come into play. If the shortcoming is due to the people in your team, it may be difficult to handle, but at least you can follow the procedure just described. But suppose your team – or even the whole organisation – fails to meet its goals and targets through no fault of its own? Perhaps the goals were over optimistic in the first place (and remember they should have been set to stretch the organisation even in the best of times) or perhaps market forces intervened. Now you face what is perhaps the most demanding leadership task of all.

In such a situation the following points are worth remembering:

1. Keeping the full commitment of your team in tough times is your job and nobody else's. People need encouragement, not punishment. Hardly anything ever goes exactly to plan, but the evidence that organisations who do plan are more successful than those who don't is overwhelming.
2. Remind people of the positive things achieved, and the positive actions which are being taken to put things right. If emergency actions are to be taken put the message over with enthusiasm.
3. **Never** avoid responsibility. Never say 'We failed to meet our goals because the silly people "up there" set them wrongly.' If you do that you are undermining yourself and your people will no longer look upon you as their leader. Furthermore you will have done nothing to rectify the situation.

4. In dealing with individuals, remember that failure is depressing. People can lose heart if they see no prospect of achieving their goals. You may need to increase the frequency of your one-to-ones for a while, and you may need to amend the targets you have set.

5. After a heavy defeat the competent football manager urges the team to 'keep their heads up' as they walk off the field of play. This is primarily because the manager is already planning for the next game, and needs to preserve good morale. So don't allow heads to drop, and think of all the positive ways you can boost their morale.

Summary

- Most people perform reasonably most of the time.
- Sometimes things go wrong.
- Informal discussion at your one-to-one is necessary.
- The key skills are **listening** and **questioning**.
- Decide whether it is a training issue or a rewards issue.
- It is not yet a formal disciplinary interview.
- When things are going badly people need encouragement not punishment – keep their heads up!

9

Managing Team Performance Reviews

A team performance review involves simply getting people together in their work teams to discuss performance and how it can be improved.

If you already hold regular team meetings or team briefings, then you are at least some of the way there. If your team briefings have become a dull routine then emphasising the review of performance will beef them up.

In reviewing team performance the team leader is sharing his/her goals and targets with the team – the very people who in most instances are going to carry them out. But it also involves listening to the team. It must be a two-way process.

These meetings are therefore not for cascading information from the top of the organisation to the bottom (though occasionally it can provide an opportunity to pass on messages from above whilst the team is together). And they are not for allocating targets to individuals either; that is done at the regular one-to-ones. Use the key result areas to provide the discussion headings for your team meetings.

Team performance reviews must be held regularly, not just when you have a problem or when things are going badly. In most organisations they take place at least monthly, but you may find that you will need to hold them on a weekly or fortnightly basis.

Meetings should be scheduled several weeks or months ahead and entered in your diary. This does not mean that the entire organisation has to stop because you've decided to communicate. It does mean you should plan for communications. However, organise them around the needs of your customers, not the other way round.

The whole team attends the meeting. If it is more than twenty strong, split it into two and meet each group separately. Managers may also need to arrange more than one meeting if there is a shift system or if certain operations must continue while people attend a meeting.

Why Have Team Performance Reviews?

We run effective team meetings for the same reason that directors have board meetings. We must review our performance as a team and we must set our sights on the future. There are other benefits too, and from time to time managers need to be reminded of them:

- Reinforcing teamwork
  This ought to be obvious! There are numerous sporting examples where triumph or disaster has been directly linked to whether they played as a team or not. Team Meetings enable the manager to manage his or her team **as a team**.

- Raising staff commitment
  At team meetings the 'why' as well as the 'what' can be explained. Employees are much more likely to be committed if they can understand **why** they will be working in a particular way as well as **what** they will be doing. Hearing the explanation from the supervisor or manager has a greater impact that any written presentation, no matter how carefully worded.

- Reducing misunderstandings
  If team and individual targets are stated at a team meeting at which questions can be answered on the spot, it is easier for each team member to know the contribution he or she and the others have to make.

- Managing change
  Employees kept regularly informed will be more likely to accept changes. Contrast this with organisations that only hold meetings in times of crisis.

- Fighting the grapevine

The grapevine never says anything good about the organisation. It will flourish and fill any vacuum in communications. The more you keep people informed at regular meetings the more the grapevine can be kept under control.

■ Monitoring morale

Regular team meetings keep managers aware of the feelings of the staff.

■ Building trust

If managers are seen to listen and to respond, this builds a greater trust and confidence in management.

The Four 'Ps'

If you are familiar with team briefing you will be aware of these headings. They help you to structure your discussion:

PROGRESS	Our achievements. What we have done so far towards achieving our team aims (goals and targets). It is a good idea to open your meeting with Progress because it creates a positive atmosphere.
POLICY	New policies, guidelines, internal procedures etc.
PEOPLE	Any relevant matters affecting staff members which will strengthen the team, e.g. individual achievements.
POINTS FOR ACTION	What needs to be done in the future to bridge the gap between our progress (achievements) and our aims, and any

special points for action which you have to discuss with the team.

It is in the discussion of action points that the two way exchange of ideas is mainly achieved. Then anything required by senior managers to be passed on is added, and finally the leader deals with other matters of local or social interest.

REVIEWING TEAM PERFORMANCE				
THE KEY RESULT AREAS				
	Quality	Costs	Time/ Deadlines	Customer Satisfaction
PROGRESS				
POLICY				
PEOPLE				
POINTS FOR ACTION				

The Structure of Team Performance Reviews

Who does what in team performance reviews obviously depends on your structure, who the team leaders are, and who is accountable for the performance of others. But most organisations have around four 'levels' of management:

1. First line management and supervision: chief communicators with work groups or teams.

2. Second line management: coaches, counsellors and supporters.
3. Third line management: direct the communication flow, answer questions and ensure that team performance review happens.
4. Senior executives: major messages when necessary.

If you are a smaller organisation, then the third line of management and the senior executives are the same people, and carry out both roles.

The prime communicator is the first line manager or supervisor. Nobody else can talk about team performance because s/he is accountable for the performance of the team. It is the single most important job that supervisors do.

The 'key meeting'

Managing team performance works best when the first line managers get together with the second line manager to discuss the content of their own performance review meeting. At this discussion there can be an exchange of ideas and advice about how to handle the meeting, what to put on the agenda, and what to leave out.

Second line managers need to support first line managers and supervisors. If, for example, a supervisor can't find a suitable location for a meeting, can't get access to a photocopier, or can't fit meetings into the shift pattern, second line managers should provide assistance so that such obstructions can be overcome.

It is important that second line managers do not just see themselves as 'post offices' for passing on information from above, or simply as monitors of the first line managers' performance. They must not be allowed to 'cop out' of the process and leave everything to the first line manager.

There may be first line managers who are not yet experienced, sufficiently trained or confident enough to hold their own performance review meetings. The second line manager is in the best position to handle this, perhaps by sitting in or holding the first part of the meeting before handing it over to the first line manager.

Third line managers are part of the process too. They should be familiar with what's going on below them, and be satisfied that everything is happening. They can also see that questions aimed at senior level are answered. This process should leave senior executives – if there are more than three levels of management – free to direct the operation, and at the same time identify messages of general importance and interest.

You can devise forms for preparing briefs and checking on team meetings and their feedback. Forms can also be used by first line managers to make a note of the questions that they themselves couldn't answer. However, it is much better to get the questions put straight to second and third line managers for a quick answer. Keep all bureaucracy to a minimum, and above all don't leave it to the Personnel Department!

Measuring the effectiveness of team performance reviews

Your team performance reviews do produce measurable benefits. It all depends on what you talk about. If the content isn't relevant to performance and productivity, quality and quantity then the meetings will be a waste of time.

Meetings of this kind are all about action. If you can identify action which you and your team can take to achieve improvements, the return on your investment in time will become self-evident.

Outside the meeting, first line managers can check that team members have actually understood the points covered and that they are doing something as a result.

Second line managers and above can 'walk the job' and ask employees about recent meetings to check that everything is working. Don't ask people to fill in forms certifying that they have held their meetings. Go and see for yourself!

Measuring the effectiveness in cost/benefits terms does take time. There's always the possibility, albeit unlikely, that a particular improvement might have occurred anyway. Measure the effectiveness of your effort by listing the action points you identify and their direct effect on team performance.

Summary

A team briefing is a process by which teams are regularly brought together by the team leader to discuss performance and how performance can be improved. Management responsibilities are:

■ First line supervisors are the chief communicators with work groups or teams.

- Second line managers support first line supervisors by coaching and counselling them, agreeing team meeting content and in helping to overcome obstructions.
- Third line managers check that team meetings are taking place and that they are effective. They manage the two way 'flow' of information to and from senior management.

Hold the meetings regularly, at least once a month. Ideally at the beginning of the working day or shift. Always during paid time. They should last from 10 to 40 minutes, depending on the needs of your business. Hold them at or near the workplace. Create a friendly atmosphere. Use a quiet area, without interruption.

Communicating the message:

- Plan beforehand and check your plan with your leader.
- Anticipate likely questions.
- Get the team tightly organised.
- Use your own language and examples.
- Stick to the subject.
- Answer relevant questions where you can, or arrange to have them answered at a later date.
- Use visual aids (eg blackboard or flip chart) to illustrate main points.

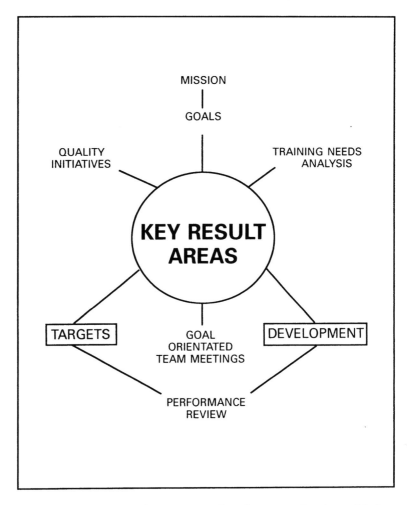

Fig. 3 Key Result Areas – The Communications Link
Between Goals and Results.

10

Sharing Goals

Obviously many of our objectives and goals can only be achieved if we get cooperation from other people besides our leaders and subordinates. There are many ways of communicating across departmental boundaries:

- Simply by going to see each other.
- Setting up interdepartmental working parties but make sure these are properly **led**. (Too many companies waste too much time on non-accountable working parties!)
- In the longer term, attaching staff to other departments to develop them, and to act as liaison officers.
- Holding management meetings and interdisciplinary training and coaching sessions.

The Goal Support Grid

Another method of improving communication with other managers about your goals involves a tool called the goal support grid (Fig.4).

GOALS

	Dept A	Dept B	Dept C	Dept D
Dept A	A's goals see page 2	3,4,16	1,9,12	8,10
Dept B	2,7,11	B's goals see page 3	9	20
Dept C	5,6,13	3,18	C's goals see page 4	nil
Dept D	nil	3,5,17	9	D's goals see page 5

SUPPORT

Fig. 4. The Goal Support Grid
© *The Industrial Society*

You simply use the grid to cross-reference the goals of the different departments or sections, recording the agreement between heads of departments on the support necessary for one another's goals to be achieved.

Attached to the grid would be a number of pages containing the following information:

- Details of the objectives of Department A, B, etc. (each department on a separate page)
- Lists of the support to be provided from one department to another, each item numbered, with the relevant numbers picked up on the chart.

The goal support drill

In order to complete the grid the 'goal support drill' needs to be followed:

- Work out your own goals for the next period (year, quarter, month, or whatever).
- Ask yourself: which of my goals and targets require the help of some other manager or managers? How much help do I need from each manager? And: what goals of other managers require my assistance; how can I best assist them?
- Explain these to your colleagues, either at a joint meeting or one-to-one.
- Agree the support (if any) needed from these colleagues in turn.
- Get your colleagues to explain their goals to you and agree the support you will give them. If necessary, seek a 'quid pro quo', and don't be afraid to negotiate cooperatively.
- Resolve incompatible goals or duplicated support. Refer up to the next level of management if necessary.
- Review the process jointly, learn lessons, and then repeat the process.

The advantages of the grid

Use of the grid brings the following benefits:

- Each manager has a clearer idea of the objectives of their colleagues.
- Each manager is committed to providing specific support, which s/he can expect to receive in return.
- Time is saved. Meetings can be constructed for small groups of people who are involved with a particular objective, instead of large numbers who are not needed.

- The manager one level up from these managers can make use of the grid to check on under or overload of work. S/he can urge the 'I've-only-got-time-for-my-own-problems' manager into greater cooperation, and the 'I've-got-all-the-time-in-the-world-to-help-others' manager into keeping their 'eye on the ball'.
- It can help in sharpening up objectives and setting new priorities for attention at the time of the performance review.
- It contributes to better budgeting. Managers can agree to contribute something **measurable** in the form of support to a colleague.

Example

A campaign requiring an income of £x could be achieved 80% through Dept A, with the remainder split 15% to B and 5% to C.

- It does not have to be implemented in a whole department or area. And managers do not even have to have the support of their leaders to carry it out effectively (though it helps); they just go ahead and do it with those colleagues who are willing to cooperate.

Summary

Follow The Goal Support Drill:

- Work out your own goals.
- Explain to colleagues.
- Agree support.
- Colleague explains his/her goals (quid pro quo).
- Resolve incompatible goals or unnecessary duplication.
- Review jointly.
- Learn lessons.
- Repeat the process.

11

Coaching and Training for Performance Management

Performance management needs to be fully understood by managers, and the methods you use to put it over will depend on your size, your resources (whether you have access to trained trainers for example) and your current situation (for example, you may already operate an appraisal scheme or team briefing routines).

The Manager's Contribution

Here are ten ways in which you can contribute to the effective training of your staff. All of them are closely concerned with performance management:

1. Determine the standards of performance required for each of the jobs you control. Set relevant goals and targets.

2. Analyse the competencies (knowledge and skills) relevant to the achievement of these standards. If necessary, seek help from specialised trainers to carry out this analysis.

3. Agree with the individuals concerned what these standards and competencies are.

4. Review with these individuals their performance so that agreement can be reached on any gaps to be filled between what they can do and what they should be able to do.

5. Every time you give someone an instruction, treat it as a training opportunity. Get individuals to tell you how they would do the job. If they get it wrong, help them to work out the best way for themselves, progressively giving them less guidance so that they learn to stand on their own feet.

6. Allow for the learning curve. Don't expect too much, but do require trainees to improve at a pace which matches their natural aptitudes. Only resort to discipline if they are clearly not trying, and have no valid excuse.

7. Give people the opportunity to learn from the way you do things. Remember the truth of the saying that managers learn best how to manage by managing under a good manager. This principle applies equally well to other categories of job holders.

8. Remember that the prime responsibility for training and developing your staff rests with you. Your results depend on their competence. You neglect your training responsibilities at your peril. And you must not rely on the training department to do it for you. They can provide advice and help but cannot replace your capacity to train on the job.

9. Plan the training of your staff in accordance with a regular review of their training needs. Take into account the principles of learning listed above.

10. Remember to use a wide variety of techniques to keep interest going.

Workshops

The best method of installing performance management is to run a series of very short, highly practical workshops which involve the managers concerned and their leaders

AT THIS POINT IN THE MEETING, SHEILA NORMALLY HAS AN IDEA. SHEILA?

in departmental teams. The workshops and the installation process happen concurrently.

High performance organisations don't necessarily draw a distinction between managers and trainers, so given some initial training second and third line managers themselves could run your workshops. The rest of this chapter offers advice about the structure of these workshops and guidance on training techniques. (Suggested outline programmes for workshops are in Appendix 4.)

Workshop Format

Performance management is not complex, but there is a lot of detail to impart. It is best to put the principles over initially in a one-day workshop. Then – and ideally after a short gap in which managers have had a chance to practise the skills – your subsequent training sessions can cover in detail:

- the techniques of one-to-one discussions;
- how to run team performance reviews;
- improving one-to-one discussions, how to share goals (the goal support grid) and how to handle special cases such as sub-standard performance on the one hand, and the high flyers on the other.

It is probably best to run them 'conference style' – with the room laid out in 'cabaret' fashion, so that groups can work together with their own managers.

Equipment should include a flip chart and an overhead projector. You will also need copies of the various forms and documents you intend to use. Everyone should have paper and writing tools.

Remember that if you have sent any documentation in advance to workshop members they probably won't all have read it!

Some tips on tutoring style

1. Avoid lecturing, or simply reading out your training notes. It is much more valuable if you can get them to convince themselves and one another of the value of performance management. This is mainly done by getting **discussion** going, either in small syndicates, or in plenary sessions.

2. As appropriate, **break up the format** of the workshop into separate sections, interchanging syndicate work, plenary sessions and individual work to maintain variety, and to keep people working and concentrating. If at any time attention starts to lag or the pace slackens, use a syndicate or practical exercise to get people going again. Do not be afraid to alter the sequence of sessions in the workshop so long as you achieve your objectives by the end. On the other hand, keep to a pattern so that people know where they are.

3. Avoid theory, and use as many practical examples as possible – from your own experience, or from what happens in your organisation – to illustrate the point.

4. Ensure that a balance is kept between the need to involve everyone and the avoidance of red herrings and fruitless deviation. Do not get into arguments – you are there to explain, not to win a battle! If someone is being really troublesome, it is better not to 'pull rank' in front of the others. The trick is to say 'See me afterwards . . .'

5. Summarise frequently throughout the workshop and recap on the points that have come out, so that the message is driven home.

6. Don't expect to convince everybody. For a few people these changes are traumatic. What is vital is that everybody gets the message.

7. Don't expect to be an expert on everything. You will undoubtedly be asked the odd question you can't answer. Don't worry. Simply say you don't know – and promise to find out. One of the others may know the answer anyway!

8. To prepare for your session, familiarise yourself thoroughly with the contents of your programme of performance management, and with whatever written guidelines have been developed. You should include additional information about performance management as it affects your own part of the business.

9. Get there early. If there is anybody you don't know, briefly introduce yourself when they arrive.

10. If you can, make arrangements for tea/coffee mid-morning and mid-afternoon.

11. Make sure that you have enough copies of the various forms and practical exercise material for your workshop.

The action session

Your workshop will have been a complete waste of time if people go away from it with little more than an 'interesting experience' in their memories! More than most management training/coaching sessions, these workshops require that your managers take specific action, action which will be monitored, not by calling for written reports, but by senior people going to see for themselves!

So you must devote time to a session covering the actions they are going to take. Take them through the action points, listing the points they make on the flipchart (get one of them to do this for you, if you wish).

This session will give you valuable feedback on the things they are still worried about (allowing you to take remedial action if necessary) and the things they have understood well which they can put into operation without close supervision.

At the end, send them away feeling enthusiastic and motivated!

Summary

- Determine standards. Set goals and targets.
- Analyse competencies.
- Agree with job holders.
- Review performance.
- Every instruction is a training opportunity.
- Allow for the learning curve.
- Let people learn from the way you do things.
- Remember that the responsibility for training and developing your staff rests with you.
- Plan the training of your staff in accordance with a regular review of their training needs.
- Vary training techniques to keep interest going.

12

The High Performing Organisation

Perhaps the high performing organisation is something which everyone can recognise, yet it is difficult to put your finger on what high performance actually is. But there are some characteristics these organisations seem to have in common:

- a sense of a shared vision (or common purpose);
- an 'opportunity culture' which welcomes risk taking;
- a constant willingness to learn as the organisation changes and develops.

A Shared Vision

The statement of values espoused by the high performing organisation is 'customer led', it looks ahead to the long term, and it is not just confined to the marketplace.

Customer led

First, the successful high performing organisation is customer led, keeping a close eye on the changing marketplace and responding effectively to change. Such organisations maintain a continuous dialogue with customers in which they listen more than they talk. The most important external evidence of the high performing organisation comes from its customers. How is the organisation perceived by the people who do business with it?

In the mass retail market – particularly supermarkets – the philosophy of 'pile it high, sell it cheap' has for many years been recognised as not nearly good enough. Of course people go to supermarkets for convenience and for low prices, but over a period of time there seems to be little difference between them in terms of price. Where there is a choice the customer uses the store which provides the most pleasant and least stressful shopping experience, and wise retail managers pay particular attention to the way the staff treat the customers at checkouts and enquiry points.

This sense of service to the customer depends crucially on whether the store manager is a high performer, a leader, or not. This is underlined when a manager moves on and his or her replacement does not quite meet the same high standards; friendly smiles at the checkout can soon become grim scowls.

When you cease to listen to customers and turn instead to an internal and introspective focus, the seeds of failure are sown, and you may have to resort to 'weed killing'. The way the staff treat the customer is an uncanny image of the way the manager treats the staff.

Example

A commuter asked a railway employee when the next non-stop train to London was due, and got the reply: 'That's InterCity. It's got nothing to do with me; I work for Network Southeast.'

High performers know that you don't get improved customer service simply by sending staff away on courses – valuable though they may be. It can only be maintained over a period of time through setting goals and targets for supervisors and, where appropriate, staff. Goals are set not only in terms of sales, but also in relation to the key result areas of customer service and quality – areas that people can actually influence themselves.

A long-term view

It is comparatively easy to achieve success in a relatively short period. While many new organisations rose and fell in the 1980s far fewer have achieved long-term success. The belief that short-term gains can be sustained provided you stay where you are is a delusion.

Investment is a key factor against which commitment to the long term can be measured. In organisations which display this commitment, research, training and development are seen as an investment rather than a cost. High performing organisations sustain this investment in both good times and bad.

Example

'Things are going really well. Do you know I'm spending so much time recruiting I've no time to develop next year's goals!'
(Anonymous director of an engineering firm)

People who lack long-term vision argue in boom times that they haven't the time for this kind of investment, and in bad times they argue that they can't afford it!

The high performing organisation usually expresses its values through a mission statement, statement of purpose or customer charter. But we all express our values, consciously or otherwise, in our interaction with customers – both internal and external – and in a way which lets the customer know whether it is today's success or our long-term relationship with the customer which we value most.

Beyond the marketplace

High performing organisations are concerned not just with their immediate marketplace, but also with the world beyond. Increasingly organisations are forging links with the wider business and social community, investing in a range of activities including helping small businesses, targeting recruitment campaigns to help those with special employment needs, providing work experience for school pupils or unemployed people, or encouraging employees to use their skills and talents outside the company.

The practical benefits of this approach include:

- better recruits, particularly graduates, as more applicants weigh up the ethical stance of potential employers;
- a better image among customers and suppliers, and improved long-term relationships;
- a chance for staff at all levels to use, develop and apply their skills outside the company;
- a healthier local economy.

Opportunity Culture

A lot is written about organisation culture, the effect it has on performance and the way old established organisations can change their culture to meet the needs of the modern world.

Some argue that organisation culture is affected by so many outside factors (political, economic, social, etc.) that managers alone, however much they try, can only go with the stream, and can have no practical effect on cultural changes. If this were entirely true, we might as well pack up and go home! In truth managers can affect the habits and customs of people at work – all those things which go to make up what we recognise as 'culture' – and accelerate the beneficial changes which outside factors also force upon us. These changes are inevitable whether we like it or not, and companies which fail to adapt will sooner or later go to the wall.

These are the main characteristics of the old culture. How many of them apply to your organisation?

- The organisation is insular and introspective.
- It is dominated by traditional functional groupings.
- Some people see the firm as providing a job for life.
- Rank and status are seen as important.
- Processes are driven by the rule book.
- People are primarily concerned with protection of earnings.
- 'Traditional' working practices are safeguarded.
- No management or employee development exists.
- There is little delegation – except for the boring work.
- The organisation is unaware of the market or its importance.

- There is no interest in growth.
- No long term planning or measurement of performance is in place.
- History or the workforce is blamed for poor employee relations.
- A general belief prevails that employees are lazy and are a cost.
- There is no systematic programme of training – skill shortages are blamed on others.

While change can be experienced as threatening, it also presents new opportunities. At the heart of the culture of opportunity is the drive to make it safe not only to embrace change but also to take the initiative in making changes.

So in high performing organisation restructuring never stops. They live in a state of perpetual revolution. You can recognise the opportunity culture in an organisation: the place is 'alive', and you can feel the enthusiasm. Such organisations also display evidence of the following five characteristics:

1. Listening

The organisation which succeeds in the face of change is a listening organisation, which constantly seeks feedback from the marketplace, from external customers and from its own staff. In this way it receives a wealth of information on which to base its decisions, and many ideas on how to carry them out. At the same time customers and staff feel they and their needs and ideas are valued. This increases their commitment to the organisation and to its success.

2. Diversity

The high performing organisation is one which embraces and welcomes diversity – in its customer base, among its staff and in their ways of working and their ideas. While it may be comfortable to recruit staff in their own image, senior managers in the organisation aim always to recruit the right person for the job. They are also willing to take risks by recruiting off-beat characters and eccentrics. In this way the high performing company increases its opportunities to respond positively to ongoing change.

3. Continuous improvement

There is a continuous striving to improve products and services. This involves aspiring to improve working practices and systems, in order that they may better serve the customer. It contrasts with the rigidly bureaucratic approach of 'old culture' organisations, where the organisation serves its systems rather than ensuring that the systems serve the organisation.

4. Empowerment

In the high performing company, ownership and responsibility are decentralised and devolved to the people responsible for the task. The style of senior management is one of 'support' rather than 'control'. Creativity and innovation are liberated, work content is enhanced, and people have greater control over decisions.

5. Risk-taking

Finally, the culture of opportunity is a risk taking culture in which employees at all levels are constantly experimenting in order to find new ways of satisfying the customer. It is through this very process of risk taking that the organisation is most likely to ensure its success, learning along the way how to quantify risk and how to take decisions about change. The risk avoiding organisation presents the illusion of security to its staff, failing to adapt to changing customer demands until it is nearly too late; and when it is eventually forced to act the changes are sudden and large, and are seen by staff as highly threatening.

The Learning Organisation

A continuous process

In the learning organisation all people are expected to continue learning throughout their working lives, whether they are high flyers on the career path, or ordinary managers and staff. In recruiting newcomers, the learning organisation not only looks for achievement but also seeks individuals with potential. It provides an opportunity for personal learning, growth and self-realisation, which is both highly motivating and also beneficial to the career aspirations of the individual. It regards research, development and training as an investment, not just a cost.

Mistakes are opportunities

The philosophy that mistakes are an opportunity for learning and improvement is an important spur to organisational growth and development. In the learning organisation mistakes are openly acknowledged and discussed, so that appropriate lessons can be learned and actions taken to prevent repetition.

In contrast, in the non-learning organisation, mistakes are immediately the subject of blame. This of course encourages people to hide their mistakes, cover them up and even to shift the blame. In this kind of organisation people work in a state of stress. As individuals move up the management tree they will feel under increasing pressure not to make mistakes, and any attempts to cover up will have even greater consequences for the organisation as a whole.

> ### Example
>
> Mistakes were costing a certain manufacturer an estimated 7% of its turnover. The Manufacturing Director interviewed all the supervisors, reminding them that their jobs were on the line.
>
> The supervisors blamed the clapped out machinery, the system, senior management, and one another. Eventually they developed systems of their own in order to conceal the origin of many of the mistakes.
>
> Now the customer is left to find out.

This approach to mistakes acts as a brake to positive change as people seek to avoid taking risks. So the non-learning organisation becomes the non-changing organisation, and as a result remains a low-performing organisation.

Fun

Success and survival in modern business is a deadly serious matter, but it can be pursued with a light heart. High performance is not a po-faced activity; it also needs to be fun. High performing organisation display the characteristics discussed above, but visit such a organisation and you will probably detect – alongside a sense of purpose, customer service and hard work – an atmosphere of enjoyment throughout the organisation, because working in a high performance company is a worthwhile and therefore an enjoyable experience.

Sub-contracting

Characteristic of the new culture is the trend towards sub-contracting parts of the business, either altering the terms and conditions of individual employees, or by selling parts of the business to another organisation or in a staff buyout. This has been common practice for years in operations like transport and company canteens, and there are many good reasons for employing staff on this basis. Indeed, some forecasters envisage the 'employee-less' factory or office. Fair enough; it can obviously have great benefits on grounds of efficiency to sub-contract parts of the work, and high performing companies are often themselves sub-contractors.

If you do this, however, you must not ignore your contractors; they are a crucial part of the business. If the airline food is poor customers will blame the airline; if your ready-mixed concrete delivery is late they don't just blame the 'owner driver'; if they are sold worthless insurance it is not just the commission-only sales associate who will be criticised.

Your sub-contractors are so important that all the techniques described above about performance management must apply to them – even to the extent of considering their individual competencies and development. So your relationship with the managers of the contracting firm must be as close as the one you have with your own managers.

High Performance and Total Quality

The total quality and continuous improvement programmes that many companies have adopted have undoubted merit. Unfortunately, however, it is possible – particularly if the organisation is of the 'old' culture – to create new procedures, systems, measurement and recording systems which alienate customers and staff alike.

Example

A company in the North West exhibits its BS 5750 Certificate in its reception area and reproduces the logo on its stationery. It employs a Total Quality Manager who maintains the various quality manuals and shows pride in regularly achieving the standard whenever the company is reviewed.

The company is an 'old culture' company, driven by rule books and procedures, not interested in developing its managers and supervisors and operates a piecework payment system ('because they won't work if we don't').

Last year poor quality cost the company an equivalent amount to its annual profit.

This company seems to have misunderstood the meaning of quality and how to improve it. To generate improvements in quality you have to get people on your side. This means looking at your existing culture and determining on change, starting with those parts of the 'old' culture which militate against quality improvements.

High performing organisations are more likely to:

- enlist their staff, get them to express their opinions and empower them to use their initiative;
- consult customers and listen to what they say;
- develop managers who willingly take responsibility as team leaders, motivating teams of people all working towards the same goal.

And all this requires performance management!

For a refreshing approach on total quality, read John Seddon's book, *I Want You To Cheat!*

The high performing team

By the same token you can recognise high performing teams. Team members share the same vision, and tend to use the same sort of language. There is what used to be called a 'sense of urgency' underlying the work that everyone does.

High performing team members show positive attitudes about themselves and other team members. Achievement, the greatest motivator of all, is apparent in the way they talk about the job.

High performing teams work hard. Team members, while having a high work rate – often putting in voluntary overtime – actually achieve more than others.

Just as there is no such thing as a 'job for life' any more, a high performing team does not necessarily keep its individual members for long. Indeed high flyers like to be in different teams at the same time: hierarchy and structure are not matters of great concern to them. And because they are achievers they move on to other things, get promoted, even get head-hunted.

And of course, whether a team is high performing or not depends more than anything else on their leader – the high performing manager.

The high performing manager

When you can recognise the high performing organisation you can identify high and low performing managers by the behaviour they exhibit – a set of competencies, only some of which usually appear on appraisal forms. Using the following profile, see whether you and your managers rate as high or low performers:

HIGH PERFORMER	LOW PERFORMER
Sets goals and targets on own initiative	Waits for goals to be cascaded down
Thinks of ways to make people more productive	Thinks of personal rewards, status, and how s/he looks to outsiders
Walks the job frequently	Stays in office
Goes to where the crisis is to help	Interrupts people in crisis and calls them to meeting in his or her office
Admits own mistakes	Blames others; opens up enquiries to identify culprits
Prefers face to face rather than memos	Always demands it 'in writing'
Has a spartan office or even no office at all	Has a posh office
Tolerant of open disagreement	Intolerant of disagreement
Helps to do the boring work when necessary	Boring work is beneath them
Trusts people	Trusts only words and numbers on paper
Delegates jobs including important ones	Only passes on low grade work
Spends as little time as possible with managers at same or higher level	Spends a lot of time buttering up senior managers
A coach who appeals to the best in people; open door; problem solver	Invisible – gives orders to staff and expects them to be carried out
Gives credit to other people	Takes the credit and complains about staff
Sees mistakes as opportunities	Sees mistakes as offences

Summary

It is characteristic of the high performing organisation that:

- there is a shared vision, which is
  - customer led;
  - adopting the long-term view
  - beyond the marketplace.
- they have an opportunity culture characterised by
  - listening
  - diversity
  - continuous improvement
  - empowerment
  - risk taking
- it is a learning organisation recognising that
  - it is a continuous process
  - mistakes are opportunities

13

Managing Reward

Example

A certain manager was told by his leader that his pay review determined that he would get *£10 per annum* less than a colleague doing a similar job.

When pressed for a reason, the leader explained, 'You are not as good at jumping through the corporate hoops as your colleague.'

Chambers Twentieth Century Dictionary defines 'reward' as 'that which is given in return for good (sometimes evil), or in recognition of merit, or for performance of a service'. It doesn't mention money.

Everyone at work receives a range of rewards whether or not the organisation has a formal policy. We tend to think of reward in terms of money, but there's more to it than that. In the poor performing company people actually decide for themselves what some of their rewards will be. Self-awarded rewards can consist of opting for an easy life, going sick, producing the minimum in accordance with the job description, letting others take the decisions and, at worst, outright criminality!

Reward for Achievement

A key part of performance management is the need to decide what monetary and non-monetary rewards employees should receive in recognition of achievement and to encourage better results. It involves reviewing the whole payment system, and of course it links with the development of managers and staff.

Performance Related Pay

Recent research indicates that about half the organisations with performance management systems also have some method of linking pay to performance. In deciding whether or not to go down this road, it is worth looking at the objectives of the reward system. Any payment system needs to achieve these aims:

- to recruit the right people in the right numbers;
- to hold on to the right people;
- to provide equal pay for similar jobs, and differentials between different levels of job – and this may lead you to consider a job evaluation exercise;
- to be flexible enough to accommodate the market rates for different skills;

- to be simple to explain, understand, operate and control;
- to be cost-effective;
- to reward good performance.

Incentives

Of course, for some people in some jobs, money can be an incentive. Some directors are paid entirely on the basis of their results; salespersons are often paid on a 'commission only' basis. Other people (in assembly or packing work) are still today paid on a piecework basis.

For most people at work, however, money is only partly an incentive. Although we all work for it, and it dominates so much of our thinking, it is certainly not a motivator. If it were, you could ignore the whole concept of performance management and go for monetary incentives instead! What we are talking about here, of course, is using money as a reward, and that is a different thing.

It's Complicated

Setting up and maintaining a salary structure which reflects pay for performance is complicated. You have to achieve the right balance between the reward part and 'basic' pay, and your system must be perceived to be fair, otherwise it will be a counter productive exercise.

If you are introducing performance-related pay, here are some of the things you should be considering:

- Are you adding 'new money', over and above your intended pay bill, or is the system intended to be self-financing?

- Is the scheme intended to be related wholly or partly to profit?
- Is the scheme to be based on individual or group performance?
- Is performance-related pay to be part of a pay increase – if so what proportion?
- Is the scheme intended to be a substitute for a usual (expected) pay increase?
- Is there an existing bonus which you are considering turning into performance-related pay?

In deciding what proportion of total pay is to be related to performance, remember that if the performance element is too small, the exercise may not be worth while, and if it is too large, earnings might become unacceptably variable, and have a damaging effect on people's morale.

If your reward management scheme is designed to pay individuals for performance, you need to decide how to measure performance for this purpose – through goals achieved or demonstration of relevant competencies, or perhaps through a combination of both?

Whatever system you use and at whatever level you pitch the calculation of performance-related pay (e.g. departmental or group), managers must have guidance on the various ratings, including information on exactly what is meant by them, and on what a model distribution of ratings ought to be.

The timing of payments in relation to the appraisal or performance review discussions is crucial. Any appraisal interview at which pay is constantly discussed and argued about will become no more than a heated negotiating session, with little emphasis on the future. It is probably best to organise pay reviews on an annual basis, linked to performance, but also covering market factors, the company's ability to pay, etc. Several organisations deliberately leave a gap between performance review time and the awarding of salary increases.

With all rating systems, there is a danger of 'drift', in which 'acceptable' people are graded 'very good' with 'very good' soon becoming 'exceptional', until after a period of time everyone is 'exceptional' and the system has lost all its value and meaning. You need to be tough on the definition of 'exceptional' and make it clear, for example, that only one in five people are going to be graded at this level.

Rating systems

Here are some methods of relating pay to individual performance:

1. *'Points Make Prizes'* – sometimes used in the more routine jobs. People are graded on their performance and behaviour and given points or gradings accordingly. These are then added together at the end of the year to produce an award. In such a system people know in advance what has to be achieved to reap the relevant reward, but it usually needs quite detailed rules, and can have deleterious effects:

> **Example**
>
> A truck manufacturer awarded grades for punctuality. When one employee was late for work in the first period after a review, he was observed to shrug his shoulders and say, 'Well, I might as well be late for the rest of the year then.'

2. Ranking by use of a league table. Divide the affected group into bands with a 'forced distribution' into each, so that, for example, the top 5% of performers would receive a 15% increase, the next 30% would receive 10%, and so on. This is a clear system, but possibly cruel, especially if the groups were very small. It would need careful explanation, with an open admission that the judgements are subjective.
3. Incremental pay scales, in which acceptable performers would expect to rise one point up the scale annually, but outstanding performers would be able to rise faster.

Poor performers and high flyers

You don't actually want any poor performers, and should therefore be taking the actions recommended in Chapter 8. A 'non pay rise' will not motivate them, so you must either turn them into acceptable performers or get rid of them!

It is the very small percentage of genuine high flyers that particularly exercises the minds of senior managers when they are considering reward management. Yet ironically the genuine high flyers are not especially interested in having their pay related to performance, because they are the ones who need it least of all!

High flyers actually need a lot more than money. They are your ambitious people and so will be looking for promotion, challenge, excitement and most of all a chance for self-development. All the other techniques and skills of performance management must be brought to bear on them, and if yours is a large organisation they need the benefits of a special programme, otherwise you will lose them!

Summary

Before setting out on a reward management system you need to consider the following ten points:

1. Make sure that the proposed payment system fits in with your organisational needs and your culture.
2. Decide what contribution should be rewarded – achievement of goals or competencies or both.
3. Establish the criteria under which performance is to be paid for.
4. Assess performance against these criteria on a regular basis. Decide on the timing of pay awards.
5. All but the smallest firms need to evaluate jobs systematically so that there is consistency and equity in the treatment of employees whose work is of similar value to the organisation.
6. Keep in touch with market rates of pay. Sometimes you may have to override your system of reward management in order to be competitive.
7. Work out the proportion of total pay which will be performance-related.
8. Ensure that your pay system promotes rather than inhibits flexibility.

9. Communicate to all staff about how the pay system works, and how it benefits employees. Consult them individually and through elected representatives, gauging their views on how a fair pay system should be operated.

10. Remember that while in the short term money can seem to be a very powerful motivator, in the longer term people need more than money (especially your high flyers) and motivation through the work itself may make a more significant impact on the performance and commitment of employees.

Appendix 1
Example of a Communication to all Managers (Engineering Industry)

[Note: In this example, the company took a conscious decision not to link performance with reward until having first established performance management.]

1. There is nothing new or revolutionary about 'managing performance' (what else are you expected to manage?) but experience shows that some proven and effective employee relations practices can be linked – or 'dovetailed' to form a coherent programme producing continuous performance improvement both from individuals and from teams of employees.

2. This means requiring all of us to agree to some straightforward drills to ensure that consistency is achieved throughout the company, and that our improvements are measurable.

3. We are therefore embarking on a programme of systematic performance management with three principles in mind:

(a) Setting sights on the future

Nothing ever goes exactly to plan, but the evidence that planning actually works is overwhelming. We need to be able to break down our goals and objectives into manageable targets for everyone, and to have some way of checking and recording our progress as we go along.

(b) Developing our people

This involves setting out a structured approach for the development of all our managers and staff to help them achieve their potential, not just 'what training courses they need'. This means having a simple process which enables people to know exactly where they stand in relation to the company and their leader all the time – not just at the Annual Appraisal – and to develop themselves and their full potential.

(c) Investors in people

We are determined to achieve accreditation as 'Investors in People', not just to receive the award, but because the programme provides us with a practical framework within which we can plan all our training and development.

4. The programme links the process of individual performance improvement and assessment with regular team reviews. It is the 'human side' of our well-established programme of Continuous Improvement. _____ – whom many of you will already know – has been retained to coach and advise those responsible for training/coaching managers at all levels through the process. He will carry out our initial training and will be available to advise all of us as we develop our programme of managing performance.

5. The training will be given in three short workshops which are intended to enable managers to:
   - Identify operational measures, set targets and assess competencies for all their individual subordinates;
   - Conduct effective one-to-one performance reviews of all their direct reports;
   - Conduct effective regular team performance reviews.

6. At the end of these workshops we shall all be equipped to:
   - explain the broad aims of the company and demonstrate how these are translated into business goals, departmental objectives and personal targets;
   - identify our relevant operational measures;
   - set relevant targets for individual staff members;
   - identify the relevant competencies needed to implement performance management in their own teams;
   - carry out regular one-to-one reviews of performance;

- set new targets and define the relevant competencies for each job we supervise and decide how effectively these competencies are being fulfilled;
- run effective team performance review meetings to **share** goals and objectives, explain the key issues, answer questions and facilitate discussion, maintain control and keep interest, and deal effectively with feedback.

7. Senior management are committed to these workshops, and the training will therefore start at the top. They will cover the whole field of performance management:

- Our corporate goals and measures – Setting divisional and operational measures – Translating these measures into targets and managing individual performance – Competencies, measuring and developing staff.
- The relationship between goals and competencies – A review of the skills of interviewing – The problems and how to overcome them – Reviewing performance and setting new targets – Discussing development using the competencies – Self assessment – Counselling issues.
- Team performance reviews – The roles of the different management levels – When, where and how to hold them – Measuring the effectiveness of team performance – Using our existing team briefings as **relevant** business meetings.

8. Nothing in the proposed programme is intended to replace or supersede the good management practice which occurs throughout the company at present.

9. This programme will help you in not only supplementing existing practice but in many cases making it even more effective. Managing Performance is **not** meant to be run separately from our other programmes,

such as Continuous Improvement or BS 5750; it will not take up massive amounts of extra time, and you will **not be swamped with paperwork**. No longer will the various types of communication between managers and their staff need to be treated as 'compartmentalised' or separate in any way. Performance review meetings and team briefings will make **sense**.

Appendix 2
Performance Management—Some Questions and Answers for Managers and Supervisors

Some questions and answers developed by a firm in the chemicals industry:

Q What is performance management?

A It's designed to help us in two ways: breaking our corporate goals down into objectives and targets for all staff, and helping the individual development of all managers and staff.

Q Isn't this just another appraisal system?

A No, it's about achieving our goals. If we don't develop our corporate plans and goals **and do something about achieving them** we will not achieve our objective of becoming a world-class company. Performance management is designed to run alongside our appraisal system at least for the time being. After a year we shall review the appraisal system to see whether it is still needed.

Q Is this just a way of disciplining people or catching them out?

A No. It is a straightforward way of recording the important things we have to do to reach the goals of the business. Many of us will fail to achieve **some** of the targets; if they were too easy they wouldn't be worth setting! But we've all got to know whether we are winning or losing.

Q Is there more paperwork involved?

A There is just **one** form, used to record both targets and staff development. The form can be used as frequently as necessary, but it must be used at least quarterly for recording performance reviews.

Q What is the basis of the system?

A Managing performance is built round the simple process of managers meeting all their staff on a one-to-one basis at least once a month to talk about their objectives and their development.

Q Will I have the time to do all this?

A Yes! If you haven't the time to have a brief one-to-one with each of your direct reports you haven't the time to be their manager either! These short sessions are intended to be somewhere between 10 and 20 minutes. They are business meetings. Many good managers do this anyway.

Q What's the point of setting objectives?

A Beyond the points made above about our competitiveness, research shows that if you have something to aim for, working life becomes much more rewarding – for everyone.

Q What's the difference between targets, goals and objectives?

A None, really. It's helpful if you think of goals as the 'long term' things and targets as the 'short term'. What happens is that the company's goals are broken down by the senior management into longer-term goals and shorter-term targets or objectives. Then managers at different levels take their own goals and break them down further, right down across the company until every employee is fully aware of what is to be achieved and how his or her achievements fit in with the overall picture.

Q Isn't the part about 'individual personal development' just some sort of score sheet?

A No. The objective of this part of the form is to record our behaviour in the form of 'competencies' so that we can make constant improvements and develop our staff. This part of the form is intended to be a personal matter between manager and staff member, and is

not intended to act as a means of comparing one person with another. It is a starting point for discussion between leader and job holder about where they stand in relation to each other.

The staff member should receive a copy of the form in good time before their first one-to-one discussion. Then each staff member should assess **him** or **herself** against the practices listed. The words across the top 'always, usually, occasionally' are intended to be guidelines, and have been reduced to three columns so that a 'clear cut' view is expressed.

Q Don't people mark themselves too high?

A As a rule no. People are often harder on themselves than are their managers. The point of the competencies is that if there is a significant difference of opinion between leader and subordinate then they have a chance – at their regular (at least monthly) discussion – to discuss the difference honestly and in confidence, with a view to identifying the areas for further development.

Q And this has to be done *every* month?

A No, of course not. Only the bits of the competencies which show we have some areas for development need to be discussed at the monthly review.

Q What about the people who are too old or too cynical to be 'developed?'

A Nobody is too old (or too good!) to be developed further. As for the cynics, you must tackle them patiently. You won't win everybody over, but by setting the right example you will make progress.

Appendix 3
Performance Management and Trade Unions

It is management's job to talk about management business just as it's the union's job to talk about union business. Misunderstandings need to be ironed out from time to time, and are best dealt with by logical discussion. Remember that:

- employees and trade union members are the same people;
- the union's role is mainly representative – that is, on behalf of its members to managers – not vice versa;

■ therefore union representatives should not be asked to be management's spokespersons.

Work with union representatives to clarify communication difficulties and ensure you understand one another's problems. Elected representatives should attend team briefings and performance review meetings just as any other employees. In that way they are better placed to monitor the effectiveness of communication to their members.

There may be areas in which representatives have traditionally been the communicators of management's messages. If this is so, the representative should always be treated with courtesy, but in the last resort the manager has the right (and duty!) to talk to his or her own people. Aim at convincing the majority of your team, not by 'gung ho' statements but through the patient application of common sense. However, if you have persistent difficulty with elected representatives talk to your leader or to the personnel manager.

Appendix 4
Training and
Coaching
Workshops

Experience shows that training for performance management is best done in short bursts, linking it closely with the practical action that managers are taking to implement the programme. Here are examples of four interconnected one-day workshops:

Performance Management No 1 – One Day

The Principles

Although it can be run on its own this workshop is designed to be used in conjunction with the other three. However, it is important to hold this workshop first, so that managers will be fully conversant with the principles of managing performance before going on to the other skills.

Objectives

As a result of participating in this one day programme, managers at all levels should be able to:

- explain the broad aims and vision of the company;
- demonstrate how the broad aim is translated into the company goals (and the strategic aims);
- identify the relevant goals at business unit level (departmental operational measures);
- set targets/objectives for individual managers and for their teams;
- identify relevant competencies needed to implement performance management in their own areas of responsibility.

The programme covers how the process of managing performance starts at the top with the Business Plan, and then how the goals are rolled down into the Operational Measures. It then goes on to show how to turn departmental and unit goals into individual targets and objectives, and finally covers measurement of performance and the development of staff.

WORKSHOP PROGRAMME

Session 1. Corporate Goals and Measures
- Presentation by trainer/manager
- Goals into targets
- The language of performance management

Session 2. Setting Departmental and Operational Measures
- Managing performance from Top to Bottom in the Organisation
- Practical exercise in goal definition
- Means of setting targets and goals

Session 3. Setting Targets and Managing Individual Performance
- Turning business unit goals into SMART goals and targets for individual managers
- Goal breakdown example
- The paperwork

Session 4. Competencies – Measuring and Developing Staff
- Measuring people's competencies in order to assist development
- Some suggestions
- Identifying competencies and suggesting developmental activities
- A summary

Section 5. Action Plan
- Each workshop member commits him/herself to a plan of action

Performance Management No 2 – Half to One Day

Running Performance Reviews

Objectives

As a result of participating in this training programme, managers at all levels should be able to:

- demonstrate how effective one-to-one performance reviews are run;
- carry out regular reviews of their subordinates' targets;
- set new targets where appropriate;
- define the relevant competencies for each job they supervise and decide whether these competencies are being fulfilled or not.

This programme gives full instruction in the skills required in one-to-one interviewing, with opportunity for role-play exercises, to managers at all levels involved in the management of the performance of their subordinates. It is designed as a supplement to the first workshop in giving further advice and guidance on managing performance and developing staff.

WORKSHOP PROGRAMME

Session 1. Managing Performance – Revision
- The relationship between goals and competencies
- The contents of the programme
- Managing performance from top to bottom
- Setting targets related to our goals
- The link between targets and competencies
- Short practical exercise
- Revision of the process of setting goals

Session 2. Interviewing: the Basic Skills and the Problems and How to Overcome them
- Review of the basic skills of interviewing
- How to run these short review meetings
- Common difficulties and how to overcome them

Session 3. Optional Session
Role play exercises in holding one-to-one meetings

Session 4. Action Plans
Each workshop member commits him/herself to a plan of action

Performance Management No 3 – One Day Running Team Performance Reviews

Objectives

As a result of participating in this training programme, managers at all levels should be able to:

- explain why team performance reviews are being implemented in the company;
- organise and run a team meeting and
  - explain the key issues
  - answer questions and facilitate discussion
  - maintain control and keep interest
  - deal with feedback.

This programme is designed to give managers the skills to hold effective team meetings with the accent on managing the performance of the team. As well as introducing the practice of regular team meetings it is intended to reinforce team briefing procedures and to help managers to make existing team briefings more relevant.

WORKSHOP PROGRAMME

Session 1. What is a Team Performance Review?

- Identifying operational measures
- Identifying the team's aims and achievements
- Why performance reviews matter – what to talk about
- Group exercises

Session 2. Roles and Responsibilities

- Why supervisors and first line managers are crucial
- When to hold team reviews – where to hold them – how to communicate the message
- Getting your point across
- How to organise and run team meetings
- Individual exercise: each group member plans and then talks for two minutes about a relevant aspect of his or her section
- Using notes

Section 3. Measuring the Effectiveness of Team Performance

- Presentation by trainer/manager
- The best procedure for ensuring that team performance reviews happen

Section 4. Action Plans

Final question and answer session, and points for future action

Optional Session 1.	Identifying the Barriers to Communication
Optional Session 2.	Team Performance and Trade Unions

Performance Management No 4 – Half to One Day

Handling Difficult Cases, and Goal/Target Sharing

Whilst all training/coaching requires systematic follow up and monitoring, managers may need special help in the form of this reinforcing session. As well as being prepared to discuss any problems of managing/performance, members should bring with them evidence of their achievements since the last workshop.

It is important that managers are fully conversant with the principles of performance management before attending this programme, and have had some experience in running one-to-one discussions. Therefore it is suggested that you run this workshop between three and six months after the other workshops on performance management.

Objectives

As a result of participating in this training programme, managers at all levels should be able to

- demonstrate how to run effective one-to-one performance reviews with 'difficult' cases – i.e. borderline discipline or grievance cases;
- explain why and how particular goals and targets are set, and review progress in setting them since the last workshop;
- devise specific actions for dealing with subordinates who are not yet convinced of the value of goals and targets;
- explain and use the goal support grid.

WORKSHOP PROGRAMME

Session 1. Revision Session

- Achievements and problems since the last Work-shops on Managing Performance
- Goals into targets: the process
- Report back on achievements and problems since the last workshop

Session 2. One-to-One Discussions

- How to improve the way you hold them
- Conversations v. interviews
- The one-to-one analysed
- Discussion of the difference

Session 3. Goals and Targets in Detail

- Why, how, how long for?: The skill of 'breaking down'
- The value of target setting whatever the context
- The importance of asking views before deciding on targets
- The importance of monitoring and reviewing

Session 4. The Goal Support Grid

- Exchanging support with colleagues
- Supporting one another's goals
- How to do it
- How it is valuable in any context
- Who helps me and whom do I help?

Session 5. Action Plans

Each workshop member commits him/herself to a plan of action.

Appendix 5
The Paperwork

It ought to be possible to carry out performance management using **just one form**. The amount of detail you put in it will depend on what documentation you already use. What follows is a possible example. It is simply a skeleton, giving the bare bones of a four-page document intended to cover all you need for performance management.

Parts of it may have to be expanded: for example you may need more space – or a continuation sheet – for the development plan.

The document usually has to be completed at least quarterly, and its contents are personal between the job holder and his or her leader. Where goals and targets change more frequently, then use more forms.

Obviously if performance review is to be used for reward management you may need to take copies of the document or parts of it for assessment purposes.

You need to adapt your documentation to suit your own terminology, the way goals are set in your organisation, and your own company's key result areas.

The first page sets out the goals of the company, the department and the section or group. The inside two pages are used for individual goals and targets, and page 4 covers development according to the competencies identified for the job.